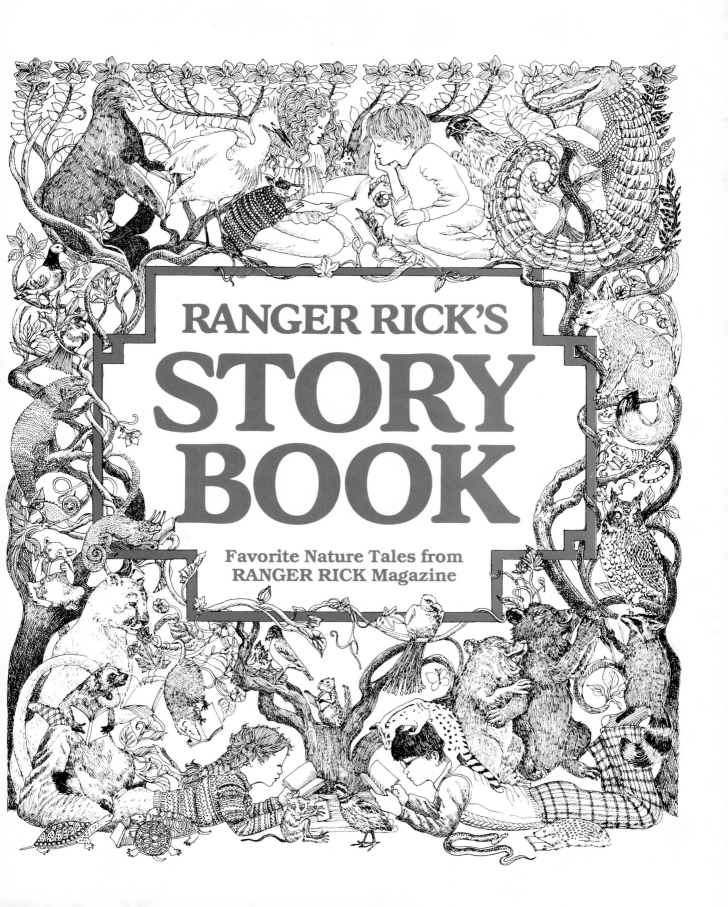

RANGER RICK'S
STORY
BOOK

Favorite Nature Tales from
RANGER RICK Magazine

National Wildlife Federation

Library of Congress CIP Data: page 96

Contents

OODLES OF BOODLES

by Judy Braus

ONCE UPON A TIME there was a village named Here. Most of the people in the village were farmers. They liked working the land, and they managed to grow enough food for everyone.

One farmer in the village wasn't happy with his farm. His name was Jag. Jag wanted to plant new kinds of vegetables and fruits. He was tired of eating the same old things. He was tired of seeing the same old animals. He was even tired of his pet dog, Rugger.

One day a stranger came to the village. The stranger was very old and had been walking a long time. He talked about a town that was far away. It was called There. He told Jag about all the strange animals and plants of There. He said the people of There had a favorite flower called a boodle. Boodles were bright red and grew on beautiful vines.

Then he described the colorful insects. He said there were huge flying ones bigger than butterflies—with spots on each wing. He also told about the field chippets, small mammals that lived in tall grasses. Chippets had blue fur and long legs and ears.

"How do I get to There?" asked Jag excitedly. "I'd really like to have boodles and chippets on my farm!"

"Well," the stranger said slowly, "I don't know if their animals and plants would fit in around Here. You see, the town of There is way over on the other side of the mountain. And things in There are a lot different from things in Here."

"Oh, I know they'll fit in, stranger," said Jag. "Please tell me how to get to There!"

The old man pointed toward the mountain. "Take that road until it ends. Then follow the path along the stream until it reaches the village. Remember, it's a long, long way, young fellow."

The very next day, Jag set out for There. He took bags and boxes so that he could bring back all kinds of new things from the village. He took plenty of food and a nice warm blanket.

After four days of travel, Jag finally reached There. Just as the old man had said, there were all kinds of wonderful things he'd never seen before. Different crops grew in the fields. Strange birds flew in the sky. And the insects and flowers were unlike anything he knew.

Jag knocked on the first farmer's door. He noticed the house was made of stone, not wood like his. A woman came to the door.

4

"Hello, ma'am. My name is Jag and I'm from the village of Here. I've come to take some of your wonderful plants and animals back to my village."

"Come in," said the woman. "My name is Mera and this is my farm. We're always happy to have visitors in our village. You're welcome to look around and take whatever you'd like."

That afternoon Mera showed Jag around. As they crossed a field, Jag noticed some large insects with colorful spots on their wings. They were just as the old man had described.

"What are those, Mera?" he asked, pointing.

"They are motflies," she answered.

Just as she said that, a large orange bird swooped down from a branch and snatched a motfly right out of the air.

"And that bird is called a gallow," said Mera. "They're always diving around the fields catching motflies."

"Look over there," said Jag. "What are those beasts?"

He pointed to two large animals standing in the field. Each one had a pair of long tusks sticking out of its upper jaw. And their legs were striped with bands of gold and brown.

"Those are rondles, Jag. They eat chippets and other small mammals."

"They sure are funny-looking!" Jag exclaimed. "But they're much too big for me to carry back to Here."

By the end of the afternoon Mera had given Jag several boodle plants to take home. She also put two chippets, four motflies, and two pet pips into one of his boxes. Pips were furry creatures with long, slender, spotted tails. Everyone in There had at least two pips.

"Oh, I can't wait until I get home!" cried Jag. "All my neighbors will be jealous. I'll be the only one with boodle vines growing on my fence! And you know, I probably could sell boodles and pips and make lots of money."

Mera smiled and waved as Jag started his long journey home.

THE FIRST THING Jag did when he returned was plant the boodles along his fence. Their bright red flowers would make the yard look very pretty.

Then he let the chippets and motflies loose in the field. He was sure they would be happy there.

But Jag noticed that his two pet pips weren't moving around very much. Jag was worried. He'd forgotten to ask Mera what they ate. "Oh, well," he said, "I'll feed them fruit—they're sure to like that. The pips are probably just tired after the long journey."

The next day Jag went out to work in his fields. He noticed that one row of his cornfield has been eaten up. *Probably the neighbor's goat again,* he thought.

As the days passed, things got worse for Jag. The boodle vines were growing everywhere. They wrapped around trees and shrubs and blocked out the sunlight. Without light, the trees and shrubs shriveled and died.

Then Jag noticed that there were a lot more chippets than the two he'd brought from There. He counted over fifteen. "I guess they have a lot of babies!" he said. He couldn't believe how fast the chippets had spread. Then he remembered there were no rondles around to keep their numbers under control. He also noticed that more and more of his corn was being eaten.

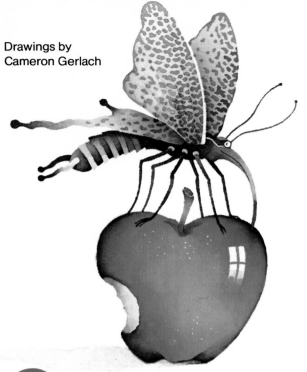

Drawings by
Cameron Gerlach

ONE DAY Jag watched one of the spotted motflies land on his apple tree. Then he saw it stick its long beak into one of the fruits. It looked as if the insect were sucking out the juice. After a few minutes on one apple, it flew to another.

"Well," said Jag, with a troubled look, "at least there are only a few of them."

Most of the other animals seemed to be doing well in Here, except for the pips. They just lay around and ate hardly anything. Jag knew they were sick, but he didn't know what to do for them.

Jag wasn't the only one having problems. His neighbor, Mrs. Piper, was upset because all her apples were being ruined by some kind of flying insect. And Mr. Murphy's corn was being eaten by strange, furry creatures.

That same day, Jag noticed a small yellow beetle chewing on the shingles of his roof. Then he saw another. When he climbed up for a closer look, Jag realized that there were hundreds of the beetles gnawing away at the wooden planks. He'd never seen anything like them before.

"But how did they get here from There?" he wondered. "I didn't bring any with me. Maybe they were hiding among the boodle plants I brought. No wonder the people in There have houses made of stone!"

The village council finally decided they had to do something. They knew the whole mess was caused by Jag and his new animals and plants. They called Jag before them and said, "We have to get rid of all those weird plants and animals you brought to Here. They just don't fit in."

Jag knew the council was right. He wished he had never brought anything back.

Jag and everyone else in the village began to dig up all the boodle plants they could find. But by now the plants seemed to be everywhere! Day after day they trapped the chippets. But the animals seemed to multiply faster than the people could catch them. The villagers also caught toads in the woods and let them go in their yards and houses. They hoped the toads would eat all those pesky yellow beetles. The people also tried to poison the motflies, but many of the insects survived.

AFTER A FEW WEEKS the villagers' luck began to change. The two pips died from not eating and were buried before they spread any new diseases. The motflies began to die off as soon as all the apples were gone. Foxes discovered the chippets and began to keep their numbers under control. The villagers made a special shellac that they painted on their houses. It killed all the yellow beetles. And every boodle plant finally was dug up and destroyed.

Jag knew he had been very foolish. But he and the villagers had learned a lesson the hard way. Here was a lot different from There. Animals and plants that belonged in There did *not* belong in Here. And that's the way things would stay.

by Robert Gray

When I was a boy, I lived in a far away corner of Montana where my father operated a gold mine. One summer a new and very special neighbor moved into our canyon. My father and I learned about her on a day in July when we found a dead deer. My father bent over the deer's body and studied the situation. Finally he rose and said, "We have company—a cougar."

He pointed out the evidence: teeth marks on the deer's throat where it had been strangled; the belly ripped open and the heart, liver and lungs eaten. Finally, the deer's body was covered with dirt and leaves. This is a cougar's way of keeping its meat from spoiling.

My heart beat a bit faster and my skin tingled. Of all the wild animals which lived around us, I wanted most to see a cougar —the *Ghost Cat* as the mountain people called it.

"Will I get to see the cougar?" I asked.

My father shook his head. "I doubt it. Cougars are very timid, in spite of the stories you've heard."

I knew many stories that the mountain people told. Cougars were said to be killer cats who slaughtered prey just for fun. According to the stories, they lay on tree

COUGAR
THE GHOST CAT

Drawings by John Dawson

branches, then leaped on their victims with a terrifying scream that paralyzed them with fear. Sometimes, so the stories went, they even followed humans, especially women. The cougars were said to cry like babies in distress in order to lure would-be rescuers into an ambush.

Oh, yes! I had heard all of those stories.

"They are false," my father said. "They are formed from people's ignorance of the cougar. Actually the cat is simply another predator who must kill to live. To the cougar, killing is work. Deer meat is its favorite food. There's a saying that where you find deer, you'll probably find cougar. This saying doesn't hold true in most parts of the country, but here in the mountains it does."

As the days passed, I found more dead deer and now and then a dead porcupine. My father said that cougars kill these sharp-quilled rodents by flipping them onto their backs and attacking the unprotected belly.

Since porcupines kill many of the forest's pine trees by eating the bark, the cougar helps nature by preying on the porcupine.

Once I found a large tree trunk with scratches on it. Our cat had sharpened her claws there. "Just like a house cat," my father explained. "That's what the cougar is—a big cat. And it has more names than any other American mammal—about forty of them. The best known are puma, mountain lion, catamount and panther.

"Cougars are one of the six species of great cats. The others are the African lion, the tiger of Asia, leopards and cheetahs from Africa and Asia and the jaguar of Central and South America. Jaguars and cougars are found only in the western hemisphere.

"At one time," my father continued, "cougars had the largest range of any American mammal—from southern Canada to the tip of South America and from the Atlantic to the Pacific. They were at home

almost anywhere — high in the mountains and at sea level, in forests, grasslands, swamps and deserts. But that was long ago. Man has driven the North American cougar back into the bits of wilderness that are left. Most cougars are in the far West, but there's a small population in the Florida Everglades. Soon they may be gone.

"Cougars are smart enough to survive — and curious. I've heard of people being followed — not attacked — probably from curiosity."

That's just what happened to me! Our cougar began following me to school. I found her tracks beside mine in the snow. I told my father about it.

"Keep a sharp eye. You might see her," he said.

Yet, as much as I wanted to, I didn't see her, at least not then. But I heard her. One night my father and I were out walking. Just as we passed under an outcrop of rock, the cougar let loose. It was the wildest, most hair-raising sound I have ever heard. It sounded like a woman screaming in terror. It echoed on and on, hanging there in the cold night air, silencing the canyon's other sounds. Then it faded and disappeared. I took off.

"Hey, come back," my father called, laughing. When I was walking sheepishly beside him again he explained that the scream had come from across the canyon. He said it was the cougar's courtship call and had nothing to do with us.

Then some months later, her tracks indicated that she was no longer traveling very far. My father guessed that she might have cubs now. He explained that cougar cubs are born blind, like all cubs and kittens. Their coats are dark brown with darker spots on their bodies and rings around their tails. As they grow, their spots and rings fade and their coats become lighter.

The cubs stay with their mother for about two years. After she has taught them to hunt she drives them away. Then she finds another mate and begins a new family.

Oh, if only I could see that cougar. It was my greatest dream. At last it happened!

One afternoon in late spring when I was walking home from school, I climbed the hill overlooking our little village. I stretched out on a rock at the top and fell asleep.

Some time later, the sun shining in my eyes woke me. I stretched and looked around. There she was! Less than 50 feet away, she was sound asleep.

I stared until I thought my eyes would pop out. Here was one of the most beautiful animals in the world—and so close! She was about 6 feet long, including her tail, and had lovely, fawn-colored fur that faded to almost white on her belly. Her long, heavy tail had a black tip and her huge paws seemed much too large for her body. Her head was small and round with little ears and a pink nose.

I leaned forward for a better look. My foot dislodged a rock which clattered down the slope. The cougar snapped awake, looked around and spotted me. I froze!

For a full half minute she lay there staring at me with her pale green eyes. She cocked her head as though puzzled by this little human who dared to enter her territory and who at this moment was scared out of his wits. Then, very slowly and with great dignity, she stood and with three graceful bounds disappeared into the forest.

I have not seen another wild cougar in all the years since that afternoon, although I have looked carefully. As my father said, they are very shy—wanting to be let alone.

It is sad that man does not let them alone. He has persecuted them for hundreds of years, hunting them down with hounds, trapping them and poisoning them. Now they are almost gone from our country and unless we protect them we shall lose these shy, beautiful ghost cats. What a pity that would be!

by Elizabeth Fritz

Mr. and Mrs. Robin were building a nest. For several days they had been flying to a branch halfway up our pear tree. As they flew, wisps of material dangled from their beaks.

From our porch we could see the nest taking shape. It couldn't have been more than 12 centimeters (about 5 inches) in diameter.

The Robin Family

Drawings by Arabelle Wheatley

Mrs. Robin wove coarse grass, twigs, bits of paper, cloth and string to make the base and sides. Next she brought mud in her bill from our flower beds where snow still lay in patches. She smeared the mud on the inside of the woven nest. Then she plopped down in the muddy nest and wiggled around and around, pressing the mud against the sides with her breast and wings. When the plastering job was dry she lined the cup-shaped nest with soft grasses and downy feathers.

The nest building took three days. Sometimes Mr. Robin perched up high on a telephone wire and trilled to warn all other robins that they had better stay out of his territory. He didn't mind trespassing sparrows or thrushes—but he would puff out his red breast and peck at other robins.

One night we heard the wind roaring through the pear tree. Would the nest be blown out? The next morning it was still there, and Mrs. Robin had settled in. We could see her tail sticking up like a flag.

Day after day Mr. Robin came to bring her food. Once we saw him astride the nest, guarding it while she

had a little outing. By craning our necks we could see four blue eggs.

About two weeks later we awoke one morning to see Mr. and Mrs. Robin flying around with pieces of blue eggshell in their beaks. The babies had broken out of the shells, and the parents were cleaning house.

We could see four big yellow beaks and the bright orange insides of four hungry mouths popping up from the nest. Mr. and Mrs. Robin pulled juicy earthworms from the ground. Between the two of them they fed the babies worms and insects at least 50 times a day.

By the end of two weeks the naked, squirmy babies had grown tan and brown feathers, and had speckled breasts. The babies were now so big they overflowed the nest. When they slept their heads hung down over the edge. They pushed and shoved each other, trying to stretch their wings.

Finally one of the babies climbed out of the cramped quarters. We could barely see him on the branch close to the nest. His speckled breast acted as camouflage. He made a move to get back in, but the other babies cheeped a clear and noisy "No!" Slowly Number One inched his way along the branch. Before he had gone very far, Number Two stood up on the edge of the nest and stepped onto the branch. As he moved away, Numbers Three and Four followed.

By this time we had lost track of Number One. Then we saw Mrs. Robin standing on the ground below the tree, a grasshopper in her mouth. Number One flapped his wings and fluttered to the ground—and she gave him the grasshopper as a reward.

At that very moment a huge gray cat sprang to the top of the fence and jumped down into the yard.

We held our breath! Would the cat catch Mrs. Robin?

Immediately the air was filled with shrill warning cries from Mr. and Mrs. Robin. Number One crouched low in the grass and stayed very still. The other three stayed hidden on the tree branch.

We rushed for the garden hose, hoping to scare off the cat with a spray of water, but Mrs. Robin was quicker. She ran along the ground, a few feet ahead of the cat, fluttering her wing. Mr. Robin hovered above, beating his wings and scolding the cat with sharp cries.

The cat paused for a second to look up at Mr. Robin, then pounced at Mrs. Robin. But quick as a flash she flew up out of his reach. Her fluttering wing had been a trick that drew attention away from the babies. We turned on the hose full force, and the cat leaped away over the fence.

It didn't take long for the young robins to learn their flying lessons well enough to go off on their own. Soon the freckles would disappear from their breasts and they would have orange-red ones like their parents'. They would find their own worms and insects that summer and fly south for the winter.

By now the flowers were blooming, and the days were warm. We were just saying how much we missed our robin family when we looked up into the pear tree and saw Mrs. Robin's tail sticking up like a flag from the nest. She was nesting again. From above came Mr. Robin's cheery song. Soon we would see a second family of robins born, raised and sent out into the world.

16

The eagle and the lamb

by Rosemary Sakajian

Pam came running across the alfalfa patch toward the Palmer farmhouse. "Ray," she called, "the eagles are back!"

"The eagles?" asked Ray.

"The *golden* eagles." Pam flopped on the porch steps and went on breathlessly. "I just cut across Old Jake's place. The eagles have a nest in that tall dead tree near the end of your woods. Same place as last year."

"Let's go see!" said Ray.

When they reached the tree, the female eagle was sitting on the nest safely screened by leafy branches on nearby trees. Pam whispered, "Isn't she beautiful? Boy, she sure didn't waste much time starting a family. Look! Here comes the male."

The children stood very quietly and watched the male glide gracefully to the nest. Both eagles eyed the children, but did not seem afraid.

"I think they remember how we watched them last year," said Pam.

"I hope not," said Ray. "If they do, we'll have a hard time scaring them off!"

"Why would we want to do that?"

"Pam, don't you remember? Old Jake swore he'd shoot them if they came back this year!"

"You mean just because he thought a golden eagle carried off one of his lambs?" said Pam. "Do you really think that's true?"

"No, Pam. According to my birdbook, golden eagles feed mainly on small animals, such as jack rabbits, cottontails and ground squirrels. I also read that golden eagles may kill a lamb when their natural food is scarce. But there are plenty of rabbits around here! I'll bet anything Old Jake lost his lamb some other way."

In thoughtful silence, Pam and Ray walked back to the house. Ray was remembering when Pam moved to the farm next door. He was glad for her friendly visits and for someone to go exploring with. They both loved birds and often watched them together. She also helped him feed the chickens and care for his pets.

As they neared the house, Ray cried, "Oh, no!" There was Jake's old blue pick-up truck. Jake and another rancher, Tony Frazier, were talking to Ray's father.

Pam and Ray got to the truck just as Jake said, "Those eagles could be back any day, now. We've got to get ready. I've got lambs and you've got chickens. What do you say we shoot those eagles before they steal another one of our critters?"

Ray cut in before his father could answer. "Eagles hardly ever attack farm animals. That's what it says in my birdbook."

Old Jake snorted. "I don't care what your book says, boy. I saw an eagle carry off one of my lambs last spring!"

"But eagles are helpful to farmers," Ray cried. "Your fields would be overrun with rabbits and squirrels if eagles didn't eat them."

"Lambs cost money, and Jake knows what he saw," bellowed Tony Frazier as they pulled away in the truck.

Ray kicked a clod of earth. "What a stubborn man. Why won't he listen?"

"He's only trying to protect what is his," said Ray's father. "Let me remind you how stubborn you were about Pam not returning your birdbook."

Ray blushed. He had been so sure Pam hadn't returned his book. He wouldn't even listen to her when she told him she *had* given it back to him one day when he was busy working in the barn. He had put it down and completely forgotten about it.

When Ray finally found it several days later he called Pam right away and apologized. But he still blushed with shame when he thought about how stubborn he had been. Not much different from Old Jake really. Suddenly he remembered—anytime now Jake was likely to discover the eagles were back. *Then what...?*

Later that afternoon Old Jake and Tony drove into the yard.

"I shot one, Paul!" shouted Jake. "I got the male eagle! He was carrying off one of my lambs too. But I think I only wounded him. He fell in the woods on your place. Want to help us find him and get his mate?"

Ray's mouth grew dry. He dashed ahead of the men into the woods. He had to get to the nest before Old Jake did. As he ran he remembered that eagles carry their food back to their nests where they eat it. Maybe he could save the female if he could find scraps around the nest that might show what the eagles had been eating.

Jake and Tony were close behind him as he reached the nesting tree. And there *were* scraps of food on the ground. As Old Jake came up to the tree Ray showed him what he had found—fur and bones from rabbits and ground squirrels, *nothing* from a lamb!

"That doesn't prove a thing, boy," said Jake. "I saw what I saw. I'm aiming to get the female right now." He pointed his rifle at the eagle on the nest.

Just then a yell came from Tony Frazier.

Jake lowered his gun as Ray ran to where Tony was standing. At the same time, Ray's father drove up in his truck. Startled, the female eagle flew away.

Tony had found the wounded male. The male eagle struggled as he held it with his heavy leather gloves. There was blood on its left wing.

Just as Jake arrived, Ray spotted something on the ground that made his heart leap. He jerked his head toward it. "There's your lamb! A freshly killed rabbit!"

Quietly Ray's father said, "So far the evidence is in favor of the eagles, Jake."

Old Jake hesitated, then said, "Well, *this* time it was a rabbit, but last year . . ."

Drawings by Marvin Friedman

Just then they heard Pam calling, "Ray, I found a lamb!" She came running toward them. "I heard a shot, so I cut across Jake's place to get here as soon as I could. I passed some thick bushes and heard a lamb cry. There's a deep wide crack between some rocks behind the bushes. A lamb is stuck down there!"

Tony and Ray placed the wounded eagle in a crate they had taken from the back of the truck. Together they carried it gently as everyone followed Pam to where she had heard the lamb's cry.

"The flock was feeding in this pasture this morning," said Old Jake quietly. "Guess the lamb must have wandered off and fallen in here."

As Old Jake lifted his lamb out, something caught his eye. He moved some leaves and matted vegetation. Underneath was the skeleton of a lamb!

"If you fill in that hole," said Ray's father dryly, "your lamb-losing days will be over."

Old Jake's face turned red. "I'll tell you what, boy," he muttered to Ray. "You and Pam take that eagle back to the truck. I'll drive you to the vet. He'll know how to treat that wounded wing." Then he shook his head. "Sometimes a man can be sure he's right and still be dead wrong.

He turned and looked at Ray and the wounded eagle, "Ok, let's get going," he said.

By shooting the male eagle, Old Jake was breaking a law called the Bald Eagle Protection Act. This law was passed to protect *both* the bald eagle and the golden eagle. It says that a person may not shoot, poison, capture or disturb an eagle in any way. If a person thinks that a golden eagle is killing his livestock, he can ask for a permit from the U.S. Government to shoot it. (Southern bald eagles are an endangered species and can *never* be shot.) Before the government gives out such a permit, it must have proof that the eagle is doing damage and that there is no other way to stop it. Since there usually are other ways of stopping the eagles from killing livestock, very few of these permits are given out.

Like Jake, many people don't care whether they have proof and don't bother trying to get a permit. Until these people learn to obey the law, the eagles will not be safe.   *R.R.*

by Robert H. Redding

Naput and his sister, Nadeen, were hiking on the tundra. It was March and snow covered the ground. For the Eskimo children, March was still a winter month.

"I wish there were something to see," said Naput gloomily.

"So do I," agreed his sister. "This hike isn't much fun."

In the distance the chimneys of their village were smoking. A breeze was blowing, and the children snuggled deeper into their parkas for warmth.

"Father said there are arctic foxes out here," muttered Naput. "I see nothing of the snow dog."

"Maybe their fur is so white it is impossible to see them," said Nadeen.

The children squinted against the sun. For as far as their eyes could reach, there was nothing but the glare of the snow-covered tundra.

"Let's go back," said Nadeen. "Maybe we'll find something interesting to do at home."

The children turned and headed toward the village. Unknown to them, a pair of black eyes watched their every move.

THE DAY NOTHING HAPPENED

The eyes belonged to an arctic fox. She had hurt her foot on the arctic ice and was limping, for the wound was painful.

As the children made their way, the fox managed to keep pace. She was small enough that tundra hummocks hid her. There was a purpose in her vigil. Her injury left her unable to hunt. She couldn't keep up with *nanuk* the polar bear either. Sometimes *nanuk* left scraps from his own hunts, and the fox ate well. But right now the bears were all out on the ocean ice, and the little white fox hadn't followed. She was very hungry. She would perish if she didn't eat in a short while.

There was one immediate hope for the fox. Had the children brought something to eat? The fox had been near humans before and had dined on leftovers. She crouched low and followed with halting steps.

Farther out on the tundra was another animal. It was *kavik*, the wolverine. His fierce, dark eyes glittered as they watched the fox. He, too, was hunting. Lemmings were scarce. There were no rabbits, and *sik-sik,* the ground squirrel, was still underground in his long winter's sleep.

To *kavik,* the fox looked good to eat. He saw that the snow dog was hurt. She would be quick and easy prey.

Naput and Nadeen ambled along. They studied the frozen snow and wondered why it made a crunching sound under their *mukluks.* They thought of exciting things to see on television. Naput remembered his favorite program would be on that evening. The day wouldn't be entirely lost.

The children paused to rest. When they stopped, the fox also stopped. The only one who didn't stop was the wolverine. He advanced craftily, his mind on one thing: Catch the fox; catch his dinner. Belly close to the ground, the wolverine moved forward in his odd, humping gait, and the distance shortened.

Kavik paid little attention to the children. They did not frighten him. Nothing frightened *kavik*, for though he was not large, he was a mighty hunter.

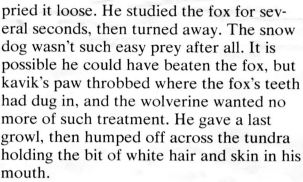

The children started home again, going a little faster. The sun was lowering, and it would be dark soon. They didn't speak, and the silence was great around them, but neither Naput nor Nadeen heard the fox. In spite of her injury, she stepped along as lightly as a bird.

Suddenly the snow dog stopped. She turned swiftly, the hair on her back raised, just in time to meet the wolverine in a head-on clash.

There followed a fierce battle. The wolverine gripped the fox by the tail. At the same time, the fox bit into *kavik's* foot. Then began a fierce tug of war, and as the animals swayed, one fighting for his dinner, the other for her life, they growled deeply.

All at once the tip of the fox's tail came loose, and the wolverine fell back. The fox scampered off a few yards. Her teeth were bared, her eyes bright with hurt and fear.

Kavik gripped the piece of tail firmly in his jaws. Nothing in the world could have

pried it loose. He studied the fox for several seconds, then turned away. The snow dog wasn't such easy prey after all. It is possible he could have beaten the fox, but kavik's paw throbbed where the fox's teeth had dug in, and the wolverine wanted no more of such treatment. He gave a last growl, then humped off across the tundra holding the bit of white hair and skin in his mouth.

The fox stood like a statue, eyes on her enemy. When she felt safe, she lay down to lick her wound. Her courage had saved her life, but she was still hungry, and starvation was still waiting. She would rest awhile, then go into the village. Her nose told her food scraps were available. She would have to be careful, because the village dogs were troublesome, but she had to try. It was her last chance for survival.

Naput and Nadeen reached their warm house. Inside, their father, Nilliguk, was carving walrus ivory into a small seal.

"What did you see on the tundra today?" he asked.

"Nothing, father," replied Naput wearily. "We didn't see a thing."

"Sometimes," added his sister, "the tundra can be very boring. Nothing ever happens."

But Nilliguk, wise in the ways of the arctic, smiled and said, "On the tundra it is what you *don't* see that is the most exciting."

Naput scratched his head, puzzled. There were times, he thought, when his father spoke in riddles.

DEFENSE OF HILL CASTLE

by Pat Decker Tapio

"Ta-ra-ta-ra-ta-ra!"

The alarm rang throughout the court as soldiers scrambled to their battle positions. Workers left their jobs and either ran to join the soldiers or scurried for cover. Castle servants hurried to protect the queen.

What is it this time? they wondered, though it didn't really matter. They knew only that a new threat had come to Hill Castle.

One of the soldiers took time to pass the message along. It spread rapidly: **"A dragon is on its way to Hill Castle!"**

Dragons were not common, but then they weren't uncommon either. It was just one of the dangers of building a castle on the desert. The dragons lived in the rocks and quite often they attacked Hill Castle. They preferred not to face the fierce soldiers of the castle, but hunger drove them to it.

Now another dragon was on his way. The ground shook as he came nearer. From the top of the hill, the soldiers could be seen marching toward the monster. They never stopped—even though a forked tongue slithered from the reptile's mouth and his scaly tail switched from side to side.

The soldiers marched closer and closer. The dragon's sharp eyes glittered as he neared them. The sharp claws on his feet gleamed wickedly. Without hesitating, the soldiers walked straight at the beast and attacked.

The first hundred soldiers were licked up by the beast's tongue. Several hundred more were squashed under his feet. But more soldiers kept coming and soon they overcame the monster. He roared his pain and fury as they attacked again and agai[n]. He licked and squashed a few hundred more, then turned around and plodded away toward the roc[ks].

At least the drago[n] had not destroyed their castle—he ha[d] not even gotten past the outer limits. Dragons were easier to deal with than giants!

The soldiers picked up their dead and wounded and started marching back to Hill Castle. It was all in a day's work for them.

Back at the castle, life was returning to normal. The soldiers had defeated the dragon. The castle was safe! Soon it was all as if nothing had happened. The builders left their shelters and resumed working on the castle's walls. The nurses bustled about the nursery. The workers returned to guard the seeds stored in the castle's underground storerooms. Grain-hunters went back to work outside the castle walls, gathering seeds and carrying them to the castle.

Several weeks passed. The castle hummed with activity. The weather was warm and inviting and many workers climbed to the top of Hill Castle to soak up the desert sun. Soon it would be too hot to come outside.

Suddenly the sun was blotted out! A dark shadow fell over Hill Castle. The workers fled in panic as the message went out: **"A giant is coming!"**

Quickly the army gathered. Many workers hurried to join the soldiers. Survival was clearly at stake this time! Giants move swiftly, unlike the slow-moving dragons. The very size of their enormous feet could destroy weeks of building in one swift kick. The army gathered together in desperate but orderly haste. They swiftly marched out to meet the giant.

But before they could attack, the giant's foot stepped on part of the castle and flattened it until there was only a small mound of earth to show where it had been. The soldiers quickly swarmed over the

booted foot and on up the leg, climbing without fear or thought of safety. Once up the boot, they crawled down inside and began attacking the giant's flesh.

"Ouch!" screamed the giant, with a voice that boomed like a hundred cannons.

His huge hand swept down over his boot, scattering dead and wounded soldiers right and left. The fierce attack inside the boot continued, soldiers slashing, ripping, tearing, piercing any bit of flesh they could reach. The giant tore off his boot and brushed away the last of the soldiers; but now his other leg was under attack.

Muttering angrily, he finally stomped away from Hill Castle. He picked off soldiers and threw them on the ground as he walked away. The ground trembled as he departed, but gradually the sun shone brightly on the soldiers and full upon the castle. Already it was under repair as the soldiers, tired and weary, marched back with their wounded and dead comrades. Another victory was theirs. Hill Castle was safe again— but for how long nobody knew.

In the weeks to come, the defenders of Hill Castle would fight off an attack by a neighboring army, travel far afield in search of food, and face the terrible heat of the desert summer.

But defending their home, fighting enemies and protecting their queen were all a way of life for the harvester ants.

Bernard Sets Up Housekeeping

by Anne Hanley

Once there was a crab named Bernard. All the other crabs on the ocean floor where Bernard lived had nice shiny shells. Bernard could hardly wait until he got old enough to grow a nice shiny shell of his own. He waited and waited and waited. But nothing happened. No shiny shell grew. Bernard wanted a shell so badly that he tried to hide behind a snail shell, but it walked away.

Now even Bernard, young as he was, knew that snails don't walk, but just kind of slide. Bernard was so curious about the walking snail that he knocked on it with his claw. *Knock, knock.*

No one answered. He tried again, harder. *KNOCK! KNOCK!* Finally a corner of the shell lifted and two small eyes on the ends of two stalks peered out.

"Want to fight? Want to fight?" squeaked a tiny voice.

"No," said Bernard, "I just want to find out *what you are.*"

"*Who* are *you?*" asked the tiny voice.

"I'm Bernard, a crab without a shell."

The voice inside the shell began to laugh. It laughed so hard that the whole shell shook, and finally it fell over on its side.

"Come out of there this minute!" yelled Bernard, who didn't like to be laughed at.

Drawings by Arabelle Wheatley

26

"Promise you won't try to take my shell," said the voice.

"Of course not," Bernard said. "What would I want with your silly shell?"

The creature laughed and stuck out two orange claws.

They looked just like Bernard's claws—the right one a little bigger than the left one. Then came a head, four long legs and four short ones. And finally it pulled out its long, soft, banana-shaped tummy. The creature looked just like Bernard, only bigger.

"My word!" said Bernard. "You're not a snail! You look just like a crab! What kind of a creature *are* you?"

"Well, we're both hermit crabs," said the creature, still laughing.

"You don't have a nice shiny shell either," said Bernard, with great satisfaction.

"Of course not. Hermit crabs don't grow their own shells. We live inside empty snail shells. And now, Bernard, if you'll excuse me, I feel terribly nervous out here."

And with that, the crab climbed back into its shell.

"Wait!" yelled Bernard. "Where can I find a shell to live in?" Bernard shook and shook the shell, but there was no answer. Then two

pairs of legs came out and the shell slowly walked away.

Bernard started house hunting, but every shell he found was occupied, either by a live snail or by another hermit crab.

Finally he found an empty snail shell, but it was very small. He crawled in headfirst to look around. He was stuck! He pushed the shell with both his claws and all his feet. He pushed and pushed. Finally the tight shell popped off.

"Now how did that other crab do it?" he wondered. He stood back a minute to think. "If I go in backward, I'll come out frontward. Yes, that must be the right way to do it!"

Bernard tried backing into the tiny shell, but he still didn't fit.

Then he noticed a bigger shell nearby. He climbed out of the tiny shell and into the bigger shell—tummy first, then feet, then head. His new house fit perfectly!

He strutted up and down, stopping to admire his reflection in a scallop shell lined with shiny mother-of-pearl. Then he saw a huge shell! It had more designs and lots of pretty colors. He climbed into it, but this shell was so huge and so heavy, he could barely move.

Bernard decided to try on a few more houses. He was having a grand time — until he saw a starfish slithering up behind him. (Starfish like to eat hermit crabs.) Quickly Bernard ran back to the shell that fitted him perfectly. He crawled into it just in time!

Since shells don't have doors, Bernard held his big right claw in front of the entrance to close it off. He got his claw up just as the starfish was covering his shell and his claw with hundreds of tiny tube feet.

Now a starfish's feet work something like little suction cups. They stick to things and hold tight. The starfish stuck its feet all around Bernard's shell and pulled. Bernard curled his tummy around the inside of the shell and held on tight with his small rear legs. The starfish kept pulling, but Bernard kept holding. Finally the starfish gave up.

When the pulling stopped and Bernard thought it was safe, he peeked out. *Better to have a house that fits. Why, that one shell*

was so big, I wouldn't have been able to hold on tight. I would have been eaten out of house and home! he thought, laughing at his own joke.

He started walking along the ocean floor to show off his new house to the other crabs. He walked a little way and discovered a pretty flower growing on a rock.

"I think I'll decorate my house and really show off to those other crabs," he said to himself as he picked the flower.

Bernard had no sooner put the pretty orange sea flower on his roof than he heard a tiny voice. "Hi," said the tiny voice, "I'm Annie, and I'm glad to be your buddy."

Bernard pushed his head out farther and stretched his eye stalks, trying to get a peek at his roof. "I don't believe it," said Bernard, "a talking flower that thinks I'm her buddy."

"I'm not a flower," said Annie. "I'm a sea anemone, and I should think you would be glad to have me for a buddy."

"And just why should I be glad to have you for a buddy?" he asked.

She waved several long, feathery, white tentacles near one of Bernard's eyes. "You'll find out soon enough," she said in a teasing but friendly voice.

"Well, I guess I'll let you ride along for a little while," said Bernard, who wasn't sure he was doing the right thing.

Annie settled down comfortably on Bernard's shell. Her white tentacles swayed back and forth like flowers in a breeze.

"I don't think I like the idea of a talking anemone living on my roof," mumbled Bernard after a while. "I'll get rid of her soon enough. As soon as I see a new shell, I'll ditch this one, climb into the new one and run away without her."

Bernard stopped to chew on a piece of old seaweed. As he chopped away with his claws, tiny pieces floated up toward Annie.

Bernard suddenly spied Annie stuffing tiny pieces of seaweed into her mouth with her busy tentacles.

"Well," he grumbled, "not only is she a talking anemone, but she's a freeloader as well!"

A little while later, he spied an empty, plain-looking whelk shell. *It's a little less than I have now,* he thought, *but I'll take it, just to get away.*

He was just about to make a run for it when Annie yelled out, "Starfish!" Bernard retreated into his shell as far as he could. Annie began waving her tentacles furiously. Bernard stayed very still. He peeked between his claws to see the starfish creeping closer. It was huge! Bernard thought he was finished this time — he would never be able to outmuscle *this* starfish.

Just as Bernard was thinking about what a short life he had had, he saw the starfish scurrying away as fast as its five arms could carry it.

"You can come out now," whispered Annie.

"What in the world happened?" gasped Bernard.

"See these tentacles? They can sting! I can use them to scare away *all* your enemies — octopus, squid and starfish. How about it, can I stay?" asked Annie.

Bernard was still too nervous to talk, but he waved his claw up and down to mean, "Yes, you can stay."

When Bernard calmed down, he started to think. *If one anemone can scare away a starfish, just think how safe I'd be with a bunch of anemones on my shell!* So he crawled around gathering anemones until his shell was covered with them.

And Bernard and his mobile home and his anemone friends are probably to this very day still together on the ocean floor.

TRASH MASHER

by Sandra L. Markle

A big alligator floated in the greenish water of a canal in Florida. Only its bulging eyes and bumpy nostrils stuck up above the surface.

Under the water the alligator's stubby legs paddled slowly. Its long, powerful tail swished gently back and forth, pushing the 10-foot (3-m) gator silently forward.

Then with a burst of power, the gator rose up in the water. Its tail whipped hard to the right. This threw the alligator's body into a curve and made a big wave in the water. The gator's mouth opened wide as the wave swept an empty soft drink can into it.

As its teeth crunched down on the metal, the alligator sank back down into the water. Still crunching, it paddled toward shore.

"There goes old Trash Masher," said Forest Ranger George White as he lifted his canoe paddle out of the water. His new helper, Ranger Glenn Carlson, also stopped paddling. Both men were on patrol for the U.S. Forest Service in southern Florida. They watched the alligator crawling up onto the muddy bank.

Ranger George knew alligators well. It wasn't unusual for an alligator to eat chunks of drifting wood, floating cans and bottles and even rocks. He knew that junk helped grind up an alligator's food, which it swallows nearly whole. But this old female never seemed to get enough trash. She attacked floating garbage with the same hunting skill that she would use on a turtle, fish or water bird.

"I sure hate the thought of getting rid of that big old gator," said George. "But she's got to go."

"I thought the people who live along this canal liked to watch Trash Masher eat litter," Glenn said. "How come she has to go?"

George began to paddle again slowly. "People did like her when she was smaller," he said. "They even threw her food and trash to eat. But now that she's full-grown, Trash Masher has a much bigger appetite. People have started to complain about her. When she comes on land she goes from house to house, knocking over trash cans and tearing into bags of garbage. I guess that shows what happens when people make friends with an alligator."

Glenn nodded. "So now the people want us to move Trash Masher into Everglades National Park, right?"

"Exactly," said George. "We'll wait until Trash Masher goes to sleep. Then we can sneak up behind her and toss this loop of rope over her mouth. All of a gator's biting strength is in *closing* those big jaws, not opening them. So once the loop is tightly in place, she won't be able to

snap at us. We should be able to get her to follow the canoe like a dog on a leash."

Glenn looked doubtful. "I don't know. What if she charges us when we try to catch her?"

"She probably won't, but just in case I brought a tranquilizer gun," George answered. "If we have to put her to sleep, we can call for extra help and a truck to move her."

The two rangers drifted a little while longer, watching and waiting. Trash Masher finally settled down to sleep on the warm, muddy bank of the canal.

Quietly the rangers eased the canoe against the shore and got out. They stayed downwind of Trash Masher so she wouldn't pick up their scent. Glenn carried the loaded tranquilizer gun. Inside it was a dart full of a sleeping drug, with a strong point on the end. When fired, the dart would jab the alligator and pump the drug into it.

George carried a long bamboo pole. A rope stretched the length of the pole and ended in a loop big enough to fit over the gator's mouth.

While Glenn watched, George carefully approached the sleeping alligator. Closer and closer he moved, one step at a time. Leaning forward slightly, he started to reach with the bamboo pole toward the gator's long snout.

Suddenly Trash Masher's eyes blinked open. With surprising speed the gator rose to her feet, flipped her mighty tail around and turned toward the rangers. She opened her mouth wide and hissed. For a second, George was looking straight down the gator's pink throat!

Trash Masher bellowed, then charged. George quickly pushed the bamboo pole toward the gator. With one bite Trash Masher's powerful jaws snapped the pole in half like a toothpick.

"Shoot!" George yelled over his shoulder as he backed quickly away from the angry gator. Glenn fired the tranquilizer gun, but his aim was off. The dart glanced off Trash Masher's back.

There was no time to reload. Trash Masher was coming fast! Glenn dropped the gun, and the two rangers scrambled up the closest tree.

Like an angry dog, Trash Masher circled the tree. Her yellow eyes watched the two rangers. She hissed and bellowed.

"Now what?" Glenn asked nervously.

George shifted his weight on the tree branch. "Sit tight. She'll soon forget about us and go back to her nap."

Trash Masher did not forget. For over an hour the alligator stared at the rangers in the tree.

"She's not giving up," George said. "Maybe if we gave her something to eat we'd have a chance to get down."

"We don't have anything to feed her. We don't even have an empty can," Glenn moaned.

George thought for a minute, then pulled off his watch. While Trash Masher watched, he threw the watch onto the muddy bank a few yards away. With a snort Trash Masher waddled off toward the shiny metal treat.

As the gator gulped down George's watch, the rangers shinnied down from the tree. George picked up the tranquilizer gun, reloaded it and fired — a direct hit! In a few minutes the drug had put the big gator to sleep.

"Keep an eye on her," George told Glenn. "I'll paddle across the canal and phone for help. We'll have old Trash Masher settled in a nice new home before she wakes up."

Glenn nodded. He leaned over the drugged alligator and put his head down on her back. "Hey, George! I think your watch is still ticking."

MAPLE MAGIC

by Kay L. Harvey

It was a cold April morning. Snow was still on the ground in the Laurentian Mountains of Quebec Province.

"*Bien, bien.* This is good maple syrup weather," Michelle Telmosse said to her cousin Leon Duclaux. Like some French-speaking Canadians, they slipped easily from French to English. The two nine-year-olds walked together behind the farm sledge.

Leon sniffed the crisp air. "Tapping the trees catches the sap on its way from the roots to the branches, right?" Leon had heard about sugaring-off here in Quebec

34

Province. But this was the first spring vacation that he had visited his relatives, the Telmosses.

The horses were trotting fast. The stacked pails rattled and the horses' bells jangled. Leon grinned at Michelle. He liked her. She had not made fun of him last summer when he forgot to latch the barnyard gate. The horses had gotten loose. His cousin Pierre, who was twelve, still teased Leon about that. "City boy!" Pierre kept saying.

"What are those pipe things in that pail on the back of the sled?" Leon asked Michelle.

She picked one up and held it in her mitten. It was a short, hollow piece of metal. "It's a spile," she said. "A spout. You have to stick the spile in the maple tree. You'll see. We're almost to the sugar bush."

Drawings by Richard Cuffari

Pierre and his father were ahead, walking beside the horses. Pierre called back, "Hey, Leon! Guess how old a maple tree should be before you tap it!"

Leon guessed wildly. "Five years?!"

Pierre laughed hard. "No! *Forty* years! *He-he!*"

Michelle nudged Leon. "Pierre thinks he knows *everything!*" She smiled at Leon. "But he's right about the maples—some trees are a hundred years old."

Pierre called out another question. "Leon, what can you get from maples besides sap and syrup? *Eh?*"

That was easy. "Maple sugar!" Leon said right off.

"*And* maple butter, *and* maple cream," Pierre said, sounding smug.

"Don't forget wood, Pierre," Uncle Claude put in. "Wood for building things —for floors and furniture."

"There's another thing that makes maples important!" cried Leon. "The maple leaf is our national emblem! It's on our flag!"

"Oh, ho!" crowed Pierre, slapping his knee. "So they teach you something in the city after all."

"Enough, Pierre," laughed Uncle Claude. "You wait, when you go visiting to Montreal —Leon will teach you a thing or two!"

Uncle Claude pulled the horses to a stop near the sugar bush. Pierre ran to the back of the sledge. He grabbed a pail full of spiles and plodded off toward the tall trees of the maple grove. Uncle Claude handed the horses' reins to Michelle. She knew her job—keeping the sledge with its buckets and spiles close to where her father and brother worked.

Uncle Claude's arm hung across Leon's shoulders. "*Eh bien,* Leon. Now we will tap the maples with this auger . . . see?"

He held up a tool that looked like a drill. "I'll make tapholes."

The hole he drilled in the tree trunk was about five centimeters (2 in) deep. He drove a spile into the hole.

"And now, Leon! *You* hang the first bucket!" Uncle Claude said with a flourish.

Leon hooked the pail on the end of the spile. Then just above him he saw something sparkling in the sun.

"Look," Leon said. "An icicle!"

Uncle Claude broke it off. "It's sap from a broken twig. Taste it."

Leon took a lick. "Sweet," he said. "A sapsickle!"

All morning they tapped the trees. Michelle followed with the sledge.

"Doesn't it hurt the trees to drill holes in them?" Leon asked his uncle.

"*Mais, non!* The holes heal." Uncle Claude patted the trunk of a huge maple as if it were an old friend. "See, this one has been tapped many times."

At last Uncle Claude cried, "Home—home to a hot supper!"

As they ate, Leon proudly told Aunt Cecile, "We tapped more than a hundred trees today."

"Good!" said Aunt Cecile. "*Très bien!*"

The next morning they all walked to the sugar bush. Leon was the first to reach the maples. "Sap's running!" he shouted. The thin, pale sap was dripping slowly from the spile. Leon dipped his finger and tasted. "It's just sweet water," he said. "It doesn't taste anything like maple syrup!"

"It will when it's boiled," said Uncle Claude. "Tomorrow, *mes enfants*, we'll make syrup!"

Early next morning they loaded the sledge with empty milk cans. Off they went, bells jingling, the big empty cans and lids clanging.

At the sugar bush they emptied the almost half-filled buckets of sap into the milk cans.

On the way to the sugarhouse Uncle Claude told Leon, "We must collect and boil sap every day now. Sap spoils quickly. In a week we might have as much as 68 liters (18 gal) of syrup!"

As Uncle Claude and Pierre poured the sap into a tank outside the shack, Leon went into the sugarhouse. The evaporator took up most of the room. It was a big, long, shallow tray. Under it was a big firebox full of firewood.

Uncle Claude turned a faucet. The sap started running into the tray. When the evaporator was about a third full, he lit the firewood.

As the fire got hotter, the sap began to bubble and thicken. Leon had never seen anything like this! As more cold sap ran steadily into the tray, it pushed the thick, hot sap to the far end. There the sap grew thicker and hotter. Steam swirled around Leon and the others. It poured in clouds through the roof ventilator. Leon thought he'd like to go out for a breath of cool air.

Just then Uncle Claude called, "Leon, *mon petit,* watch the thermometer for me! Pierre and I have to work outside. Michelle is off daydreaming somewhere. *Attention,* Leon. Call me as soon as the temperature gets to 104°C (219°F). Then we must drain off some syrup. If it gets too hot, we will not make syrup. It'll turn to maple cream. Now don't forget to watch!"

"I'll watch!" Leon promised. The thermometer had several degrees to go.

Uncle Claude disappeared. Leon walked up and down beside the evaporator. The sap bubbled. The steam swirled. The air was heavy and sweet. Leon felt a little dizzy watching the plopping, thick goo.

Suddenly Leon remembered the thermometer. Quickly he peered through the steam at the numbers. He was lucky! Almost up to 104!

"Uncle Claude!" he shouted.

Uncle Claude ran in. *"Bien,* Leon!" he said. *"Bien!* Right on time!"

Uncle Claude turned a spigot at the end of the tray. A stream of smooth, golden syrup flowed into a big bucket. Then he strained the syrup.

Leon walked outside. He was glad he hadn't made another "city boy" mistake!

By the end of the day they had 11 liters (3 gal) of syrup from about 380 liters (100 gal) of sap. And in the days that followed, they made a lot more.

A week later Aunt Cecile said, *"Eh bien, mes enfants.* That's enough. Tomorrow we'll have a sugaring-off party—before Leon has to go home."

The children cheered.

"We'll have *crêpes!* All you can eat!" promised Aunt Cecile.

"Pancakes and new maple syrup!" sighed Leon. "I'm hungry already."

The next day Pierre and Leon built a fire in the clearing near the farmhouse. Aunt Cecile put skillets on the grill over the fire. Soon everyone had a huge plateful of pancakes.

Maple syrup had never tasted so good to Leon. Just as he thought he could not eat another mouthful, Michelle spooned some syrup on a bowlful of snow.

"Here, try some *tire*, Leon," she said. "It's snow taffy."

It was delicious. But now Leon could not eat even *one* of the sugar patties Pierre had made from thick syrup, set in muffin tins.

The following morning, when Leon was ready to leave, Pierre handed him a package. "Take these with you. It's a jar of syrup and a bunch of sugar patties I made." Pierre grinned his big grin. "Your city friends have to *buy* stuff like this. These you helped to make!"

Leon also grinned. *"Merci, Pierre, mon ami."* It was going to be hard to wait a whole year for another sugaring-off!

The Owl Woods

by Jill Taylor

Just like real Indian hunters, Bill and Jimmy Cope crept noiselessly through the woods. They had small bows and arrows and were planning to shoot at pine cones.

Suddenly Bill stopped and held up his hand. "*Shhh!*" he whispered. "Something moved in that pine tree!"

Jimmy looked. "I see it!" he said. "It's some kind of animal!"

"Let's sneak up on it!" Bill said.

"There's more than one!" Jimmy said, "At least a dozen! What *are* they? They have horns—and big yellow eyes!"

Bill whispered, "I *think* they're long-eared owls! Remember the picture Mr. Wagner showed us? He said there was a flock that spends winters here in the woods."

Mr. Wagner owned the forest. He knew as much as most Indians about plants and wildlife. He especially knew about owls. The boys had spent a lot of time tramping the woods with him.

Slowly the boys circled the tree, looking up. The birds' "ears" were really long tufts of feathers. Their faces were round and the size of a cat's. Their long wings were tucked against their bodies. Their heads turned very slowly, and their yellow, unblinking eyes never looked away from the boys.

"I wish they'd fly!" Jimmy said.

"I know," said Bill. "Let's shoot arrows up into the trees, just to scare them into the air."

"O.K.," Jimmy agreed. "But I wouldn't want to hit one!"

"We couldn't hit them if we tried!" laughed Bill. "Not with these dinky bows."

They lifted their bows. With a *zing* and a *twang* the small arrows shot up into the branches. Silently the owls flew off.

"Man, they're big!" gasped Jimmy. "They must be three feet across!"

"Jimmy, look!" yelped Bill, grabbing his brother's arm. "There's an owl over there *with an arrow sticking out of it!*"

The owl was trying to fly away, but it wobbled and bumped into branches. Finally it disappeared among the trees.

"What'll we do!" Jimmy wailed. "What will happen to the owl? It's hurt!"

"We've got to find it!" said Bill.

They dropped their bows and arrows in the bushes and went crashing into the woods.

They hadn't gone far when they heard a call behind them: "Is that you, Bill? Jimmy?" It was Mr. Wagner. "Hey, there!"

Jimmy looked at Bill. "He'll be awful mad, won't he!" he whispered. "But the owl. Mr. Wagner will know what to do for it."

Bill nodded. "Right. He'll help us."

The boys turned back. They found Mr. Wagner standing beneath the owl tree.

"Hi, boys!" he greeted them. "Look here. This is a pellet left by a long-eared owl. The owls swallow mice and other rodents whole, then cough up the bones and fur. See? Here are the tiny bones. One owl can eat up to one-half its own weight in mice every day. Owls are valuable." He pointed to other pellets lying on the ground around the tree.

Bill and Jimmy looked at each other.

"Mr. Wagner," Bill began, "we have something to tell . . ."

"We shot an owl!" Jimmy said flat out.

Mr. Wagner's face got very red. "I can't believe . . ."

"Hey, look up there!" Bill cried. He pointed. "The owl's back!" Then he

Drawings by Ted Lewin

40

groaned. "And the arrow's still in it!"

Slowly the owl fluttered to a branch above their heads.

"Well, I'm glad it's alive," Mr. Wagner said very quietly. "Come here, Bill. Stand on my shoulders. I think you can reach the owl and get it down from there. But first, put these on. Owls' talons are very sharp." He handed Bill a pair of very thick leather gloves. "Ready? Up you go!" He lifted Bill to his shoulders and held his legs. Bill stretched up toward the owl.

With a sudden lurch the owl tried to fly off, but the arrow caught in some small branches. Settling back on its perch, the owl hissed and snapped. Bill ducked. When he reached up again he touched the owl's legs. Suddenly the owl's strong talons wrapped tightly around one finger.

"Fine," said Mr. Wagner. "Now grasp its back. Hold it gently and try not to wiggle the arrow."

Bill carefully lifted the bird. He was amazed at how light it was and how little it struggled to get free.

They hurried to Mr. Wagner's house and drove off to the veterinarian's.

The boys watched as the doctor cut off one end of the arrow and pulled it out.

With a long, flat stick the doctor raised the feathers on the owl's body. He found the two holes left by the arrow.

"It looks as if the arrow entered the front of its breast and came out the side. It just touched the breastbone," he said. "Not much damage." He poured some white powder on a folded piece of paper. "You know," he said, "owls are birds of prey, and it's against the law to kill them. And you're not even allowed to capture them. Even hunters with licenses can shoot only game birds in season, never birds of prey. You're lucky, this fellow will be O.K."

The doctor held the paper close to the owl, and blew some of the powder onto each small wound. "Guess that's the best I can do for it," he said. "Take it home now, and feed it some of this sulfa powder mixed with raw steak and water. We don't want to risk infection." He handed the boys a small envelope of the powder. "After that, turn the owl loose."

"We'll have to get a special-purpose permit from the U.S. Fish and Wildlife Service," Mr. Wagner told the boys. "We need permission to keep the owl until it is well enough to fly."

Back at Mr. Wagner's house, they made up the food-and-sulfa-powder mix. They offered it to the owl on a flat stick. The owl hissed and snapped at the stick when it was held out. After that when it snatched at the stick it snatched at the meat too, and smacked its beak.

A few days later Mr. Wagner and the boys saw that the wound was healing.

They picked up the owl and carried it back to the owl tree in the forest. Mr. Wagner reached up into the tree as far as he could and carefully placed the bird on a branch close to the trunk. Then, very slowly, he and the boys backed away, keeping their eyes on the owl.

Would it be able to fly? Would it go off to hunt for food with the rest of the flock? After a few long moments the owl slowly stretched first one wing, then the other. Then, with a gentle push, it floated into the air and flew off.

"Whew!" said Jimmy. "What a relief!"

"Yeah," said Bill. "I was going to shoot *myself* if it didn't make it!"

Mr. Wagner grinned. Then he looked very serious. "I guess you boys don't have to be told how and where to use your bows and arrows."

"No, *sir!*" they both said.

Adapted from *Words of Cheer*, 10 January 1965, The Mennonite Publishing House, Scottdale, PA 15683.

SNOWY TAKES A TUMBLE

by Joseph J. Branney

Snowy's mother landed carefully on a nest of reeds and sticks. She bent over and coughed up some fish she had caught in the marsh for her chicks. Snowy and the two other chicks tore eagerly at the food. Soon it was gone.

Snowy's mother and father took turns feeding and watching over the chicks. Sometimes the young birds ate frogs or snakes besides the small fish their parents caught for them.

Snowy and his family were *snowy egrets*. Snowy's parents had long thin legs that were good for wading in the shallow water of the marsh. Their yellow feet were nicknamed "golden slippers."

People used to hunt adult egrets like Snowy's parents for their beautiful white plumes, or feathers. But now the egrets are protected, so the feathers can stay on the birds instead of being used for plumes on women's hats.

Here in the *nesting colony* or *rookery (ROOK-uh-ree)*, other snowy egrets, herons, and ibises lived near Snowy's family. Like the snowy egrets, the other marsh birds made their nests of reeds and rushes. The nests rested on bent-over reeds in the marsh.

When it got too hot in the marsh, Snowy and the other egret chicks crawled to the edge of the nest to find some shade. Often one of Snowy's parents would stand on the nest to shade the chicks with its wings.

One afternoon there was a strange sound in the marsh: *Putt, putt, putt, putt, putt.* What was that? A flock of marsh birds took off from their nests, flapping their wings. Frightened by the noise and commotion, Snowy fell right over the edge of the nest. *Splash!* The people passing by in the motorboat probably didn't know that the noise would scare so many birds.

Dripping wet, Snowy crawled out of the shallow water onto some reeds. He looked up at the nest. It was only two feet above him. But it looked very far away. He called as loudly as he could. His father looked down and called back to him.

Snowy tried to climb up the reeds to the nest but he couldn't. At that point it was all he could do just to stay out of the water. He was lucky that no hawks or crows knew he was there. They like to eat egret chicks whenever they can.

Snowy's mother came back to the nest with more food for the egret chicks. Snowy could hear the two other chicks in the nest. They were squawking as they

gobbled up the fish. He called out loudly, but his parents seemed to have forgotten him. That night Snowy missed his dinner. He was *very* hungry.

All through the night Snowy crouched in the reeds. A large snapping turtle swam close but went on its way. Luckily no raccoons came near enough to find out they could have a chick for dinner.

Shortly before dawn Snowy's mother flew off to fish for breakfast. Snowy was so hungry that he was beginning to feel weak. He heard his mother's call overhead as she flew back to the nest.

Instead of landing on the nest, Snowy's mother landed in the reeds next to Snowy. She lowered her head and coughed up three fish for him. The hungry chick gulped down all three. Then his mother stepped toward the nest. The reeds bent underneath her as she walked. Snowy's father and the other two chicks greeted her as she stepped back onto the nest.

Snowy was very lucky that his mother had brought him some food. Most egret parents won't feed a chick that has fallen out of the nest. The chick usually doesn't last very long before it starves or is eaten by a hungry animal.

Snowy now had eaten, but he was not yet out of danger. Though the nest was still above his head, the reeds his mother had bent gave him a new chance. He tried to climb about on the reeds, using his bill as well as his toes to keep his balance. It was hard work. Step by step, he made his way up the reeds. Although he wobbled as he climbed, he didn't fall. Finally he made it back to the nest.

Soon Snowy and the other two egret chicks would all be strong enough to climb in and out of the nest with ease. But what a way to learn!

Drawings by Linda K. Powell

SUE'S BIG FISH

by Gerry Bishop

A fuzzy little fly settled on the surface of the pond. It rested there a moment, its round red belly shining in the morning sun. Quietly and with the slightest bit of caution, a sunfish drifted upward. It lunged with a *gulp* that every creature around must have heard, and the fly vanished.

What the sunfish was about to discover was that it had just made a very big mistake. That "fly" was really a sharp hook wrapped with fancy feathers and tied to a line. On the other end was Sue, and she was ready!

The sunfish, feeling a strange pull in its mouth, had no way of understanding what was wrong. But it *did* know enough to fight! It turned its flat, muscular body against the line and tugged with all its might.

"I got one!" Sue yelled to her little brother Tom, "and he's a *monster!*"

The frightened sunfish tried diving and then leaping and wiggling on the surface. Next it darted into some underwater weeds and almost tangled the line, but Sue held on. Her delicate fly rod danced with every tug until a very tired fish rolled to the surface. Sue carefully pulled in her line until she could reach down and gently pick up the beautiful silver-blue and orange fish.

"Wow," said Tom, splashing through the mud to his sister's side. "What a beauty! He's big enough for *both* our breakfasts."

"I think we've already caught enough for breakfast, Tom. I'm going to let this one go. After that brave fight he deserves it!"

Sue had loved fishing ever since she first tied a safety pin to a piece of string and dipped it into a puddle in her backyard. Later she got a spinning rod as a present and used it until she was ten years old.

Now she had bought her own fly rod! She had bought it with money saved all winter long. And with the help of a few books from the library,

and some practice, she quickly learned that casting a fly isn't nearly so hard as everyone had told her. It is just different from other kinds of casting.

As Sue cast with her spinning rod, a weight tied to the end of a light line pulled it spinning off the reel. In fly casting the tiny flies are just too light to pull a heavy line. Sue first had to pull the heavy line off the reel by hand. Then she flipped it back and forth over her shoulder like a whip. With the last whip the line carried far out over the water—and the tiny fly, attached at the end by an invisible, thin "leader" line, landed on the surface like a live insect.

Almost as much fun as fly-fishing was making the flies. Sue wrapped strips of fuzzy wool and shiny tinsel on a hook, then added a few feathers for wings and legs. Her books showed her how to make a few fishing favorites, but she was soon letting her imagination go.

"What's that one?" her brother would ask as she finished each fly.

"That's a spider with a *hundred* legs!" she'd answer.

Even when she was trying to copy a real insect her brother couldn't always recognize it. But it didn't matter to him, and it really didn't matter to those sunfish. They always seemed ready to snatch one of Sue's flies, and Sue never tired of trying out new creations. She wanted to catch the biggest sunnies in the pond. Even more she wanted to catch a bass—and one bass in particular.

This bass spent most of its feeding time in the shallow water at one end of the pond. The water there was sparkling clear, and the bass could see every move below the water

Drawings by Frank Fretz

47

and above. By the looks of its round, sagging belly, it was catching more bite-sized creatures than any other pond dweller.

Sue was sure she could catch it with her spinning rod and a juicy worm. But she figured it was time to see just how good she was with her fly rod.

One evening she crept along the bank of the pond to one of the bass's favorite feeding spots, carefully staying out of sight. There was the big bass, cruising slowly near the bank, waiting for grasshoppers to slip and fall into the water.

Fancy feathers on a long hook make a darting minnow.

That's it, Sue thought. *Grasshoppers!* She reached eagerly into her fly box and picked out one of her favorite creations—a bristly brown fly with two large folded wings on the back. She quickly tied it to her line and, careful to stay hidden, flipped it back over her shoulder and then out toward the bass. The fly hit the water as naturally as a real grasshopper falling from the bank. That instant

Chunks of sponge rubber and some rubber bands become a spidery bug.

Sue knew she had a chance. A cool chill raised the hair on her neck as the ripples rolled away from the fly. The excitement of this moment was what made fly-fishing the greatest!

The bass turned and moved toward the fly. That odd bunch of feathers was the center of attention—the bass watching from below, and Sue from above. When the last ripple disappeared, Sue twitched the fly the tiniest bit. A flick of the bass's strong tail made the smooth water above it seem to boil. A mouth as wide as a saucer splashed through the surface and snapped closed over the fly.

Sue didn't have a chance to think. If she had, she might have wondered what in the world she was doing tangling with a big fish like *that!* She grabbed the rod with both hands as the powerful bass knifed away. The rod bent nearly double and her line zipped from its reel. Then up the bass came, leaping from the water and angrily shaking its head. On the last shake the fly shot from its mouth and landed at Sue's feet.

She stood there, eyes wide and heart pounding, gazing at the water. Everything had happened so fast that she had to stop to figure out just what *did* happen. Her first urge was to try again. But her fly was torn to shreds, and she knew that the bass would not fall for the same trick twice —not twice in the same day.

The bass, meanwhile, swam to hide in deep water. It would return to the shallows sometime after dark, but now it would be more careful in choosing grasshoppers.

Sue broke into a grin as she wound in her line and started home. She was thinking of another fly she could make to try again to outsmart that old bass. *A dragonfly,* she thought. *I know bass love dragonflies. Or maybe one that looks like a little frog. Yeah, that's it! If I could land a frog-fly on one of those lily pads, I could make it hop off just like a real one would. That'll do it, I'm sure!*

A piece of cork and bundles of hair make a floating frog.

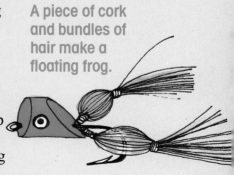

GREEN VELVET PRINCESS

by Ruth Higbie

Jessica liked to hike in the woods and fields whenever she could. On rainy days she liked to read.

One stormy afternoon she found a fairy tale in an old book. It was called "The Princess Worm." A beautiful princess had been changed into a caterpillar by a jealous, ugly witch. The witch laughed when she saw the princess crawling on the ground. She told the princess she could change back only if a prince kissed her.

"Just a fairy tale," said Jessica, looking out the window. "It's impossible to change into something completely different. Oh, I do wish it would stop raining!"

The next day the sun shone. As soon as she was dressed, Jessica went outdoors. As she ran down the path through the pine trees, she saw a big caterpillar. It looked as if it were made of green velvet. It had a row of white spots down its sides. Long, delicate white hairs covered its 2-inch (5-cm) body. Near its head was a circle of eight golden spikes. To Jessica they looked almost like a crown.

"It's the Princess," whispered Jessica to herself, playing make-believe. "She must have been wearing a green velvet gown with pearl buttons when the wicked witch put a spell on her. She was wearing her gold crown and a thin white cape.

"Look. Little gold knobs run all down her back, so she wore a long gold necklace too. Poor thing. She can be the princess in my terrarium."

Jessica carefully cut off part of the pine branch where the caterpillar was crawling. She put the branch and the caterpillar into the terrarium she had made from an old fish tank.

The caterpillar's three pairs of front legs were bright yellow. "The Princess was wearing gloves," said Jessica. Four pairs of short, soft, green legs held tight to the pine twig. So did a pair at the end. Those legs were black and gold. The Princess's long gown must have had beautiful black and gold trim, Jessica decided.

The yellow legs grabbed the tip of a pine needle. Slowly they worked to pull the needle into the caterpillar's mouth. The caterpillar chewed away until it had eaten the whole needle. Then the golden legs reached for another needle and brought it to the caterpillar's mouth.

Jessica never saw her princess caterpillar do anything but eat. Every day or so, when all the needles had been eaten, Jessica set a fresh branch in the moist soil of the terrarium.

In a book about moths and butterflies, Jessica found a picture of her caterpillar. The one in the picture didn't look as pretty as *her* "princess." The book said the caterpillar was the *larva* of the imperial moth.

"I knew she was special!" cried Jessica. "Imperial means she'll be an empress. That's even better than a princess or a queen. But, oh dear, how can a prince find her here?"

The moth book said imperial caterpillars eat pine needles and other types of tree leaves. Most of these caterpillars are green, but some are brown.

The next morning when Jessica checked the terrarium, the caterpillar was gone! It *couldn't* have gotten out!

Oh, where could it be? Then Jessica saw a wrinkled, dark green lump on the dirt under the pine branch.

"She's dead!" cried Jessica. "Now the prince will never find her!"

But suddenly the wrinkled lump began to twist and turn. It wiggled down into the soil and disappeared.

What was happening? Jessica carefully brushed away a bit of soil. Then she watched her princess caterpillar squirm and wiggle right out of its skin. All that was left of the beautiful green velvet gown was a crumpled rag. Now the princess caterpillar didn't look like a caterpillar anymore. And it didn't look like a princess, either. Instead it had changed into a creamy white "egg" — very soft and only an inch and a half (4 cm) long. Gently, Jessica pushed some soil back over it.

Two days later she peeked under the soil again. Something else had happened. The soft white sac had turned hard and shiny brown.

"It's a *pupa*," said Jessica. "Next summer it will turn into an adult moth. Most moths spin silk cocoons to protect themselves. But this one digs into the ground. That's just as safe, I guess. But, oh dear, such a long time to wait before something happens."

Jessica decided to put her terrarium in the shed. She knew the pupa had to stay cold before it could change into a moth.

Months passed. The pine branch turned brown. Jessica checked the pupa each day.

One morning when summer finally came she saw a strange shapeless thing on the dead branch. It had a fat body, and four wrinkled pieces hung down from its sides. As Jessica watched, a wonderful thing happened. The wrinkles smoothed out. "Look!" Jessica cried. "They've turned into *wings!*"

Jessica carried the tank outside. She sat down beside it and watched. The moth's body turned to yellow with purple stripes. Slowly the wings spread out and

stiffened. They were almost 5 inches (12.5 cm) across. As they dried, they became a lovely soft yellow with pale purple spots on them. A wavy purple band ran across the wings.

Jessica was terribly excited. This creature was even more beautiful than the green velvet caterpillar had been. "How wrong I was to say it was impossible for anything to change completely!" she said.

By the time evening came, the moth's wings had grown strong. Jessica watched as the imperial moth spread them and fluttered off into the dark.

"Good-bye, Empress," she called. "The magic worked! One day soon a true prince, another imperial moth, will find you. Then you will lay eggs. They will turn into green velvet princesses just like you were when I first found you."

DIRTY FACE
LEARNS TO FISH

by Richard C. Davids

The world seemed wonderful to Dirty Face, a little brown bear who lived with her big, furry mother beside the McNeil River in Alaska. She got her name from her muzzle, which was always black, no matter how carefully and how often her mother licked it.

Dirty Face didn't care. She was happy. There were plenty of roots and berries and mice to eat. The river was clear and full of salmon, and Mother Bear was a fine fisherman. She could grab a fish in her big mouth and dig up ground squirrels with her curved claws, which were half as long as a pencil. All Dirty Face had to do was watch and feast.

When Dirty Face was three years old, Mother Bear had twin male cubs. After that, life was never the same for Dirty Face. Every time she came near her little brothers—who looked like roly poly Teddy bears—Mother Bear snarled and growled. And one day Mother Bear and her twin babies walked away, leaving Dirty Face all alone.

Dirty Face was very sad. Before long she grew very hungry. She dug for roots in the sand bars but couldn't find any. She climbed the riverbank and sniffed for ground squirrels. But her mother had already found them.

Sadly, Dirty Face returned to the river and gazed out over the cold, cascading water. If

Drawings by Irene Brady

you were a little bear, how would you catch fish with only your mouth and two bare paws? Dirty Face inched her way out on a shallow reef. She saw the salmon darting past on their way upstream to lay their eggs. Dirty Face should have watched more closely when her mother had fished!

A salmon paused. Dirty Face batted at it with her left paw so hard she slipped and fell into the swirling water. She crawled out and shook herself.

In all the world there was no colder, sadder bear than Dirty Face.

But hunger made her try again. Though she was still a cub, she weighed 300 pounds. By the time she would be eight and a grownup, she would be three times that big. The Alaska brown bear is the biggest meat-eating land animal on earth. So you see why Dirty Face had to eat. Besides, she could eat only in summer, because all winter she would doze in a den hidden beneath the deep snow.

She waded out in the water and stood on her hind legs. She could see the fish better that way. A herring gull came to watch. Dirty Face stood and waited until the cold water made her feet ache. Once again she went to shore and shivered.

She bellered for her mother but there was no answer. All day she had been without food. Once when she wasn't looking, a salmon leaped out of the water beside her. The smell of fish made her even more hungry. She jumped into the river, lost her footing on the rocks and was covered with white spray.

Struggling to find her footing, she felt a stick. But it wasn't a stick. It moved. Her claws sank deep and held it—a fat, wriggling salmon!

She grabbed it in her mouth and splashed her way to shore, paused and shook herself so hard the droplets made a shiny mist around her. The gull screamed above her. This was fun! Getting your own fish was even better than having your mother catch fish for you. Being a grownup was going to be exciting.

Dirty Face learned that salmon sometimes rest before leaping upstream over the rocks, and in the foaming water they couldn't see her. She learned to feel for them and when to pounce. Sometimes with one fish already in her mouth, she would try to catch another. Often she would disappear completely under water. Now and then she would dive and go head over heels. She was in the water a third of the day. The exercise kept her warm.

It is said that by August, Dirty Face was the best fisherman on the whole river!

by G. W. Compton

On a lovely coral reef,
in a warm and sunny sea,
there was a wonderful world of strange
and beautiful creatures.
Fishes and lobsters,
crabs, clams and snails.
Sponges and starfish,
Sharks with big tails.
Seahorses, jellyfish,
shrimps and morays.
Scallops and turtles,
sea fans and rays.
A hundred feather duster worms,
two dozen sea cucumbers,
and several octopuses —
and that's not all:
The jumble of coral that made up the reef
was home for hundreds and hundreds of different
sea creatures,
all shapes and sizes —
fast swimmers,
slow swimmers,
creatures that crept,
creatures that crawled,
and some that just sat still,
scarcely moving at all.
Like one very pretty sea anemone.
It looked like a garden flower with
long white petals with pink tips.
But the Anemone wasn't a flower;
it was an animal.
The white petals with pink tips were
really tentacles.
They were the Anemone's arms.
In the middle of all the tentacles was the
Anemone's small pink mouth.
The Anemone couldn't swim —
anemones can't.
And it couldn't see —
anemones have no eyes.
Mostly it just sat holding onto a coral.

Once in a while it would slide on its bottom
to another place on the coral.
But very slowly,
slower than a snail.
The Anemone just sat and waited until some
food came along and touched its tentacles.
The Anemone caught small animals to eat wi
its tentacles.
It used them like fingers to push the food
into its small pink mouth.

The Clownfish and the Anemone

56

Each tentacle had thousands and thousands
of tiny stinging cells on it.
If anything touched a sting cell, it would
shoot out a very small dart.
Each dart was sharp as a needle,
and each dart had poison in it:
Enough poison to kill very small fishes
or paralyze them so they couldn't get away;
enough poison to hurt big fishes and make
them stay away.
All fishes kept away from the
Anemone's tentacles.
All except for one small fish on the reef,
a clownfish.
Like all other clownfishes, she was about
as big as your little finger.
She could swim and she could see.
She had no problem catching enough to eat.
The Clownfish was one of the prettiest
fishes on the reef.
Like many other clownfish,
she had a plump little body,
black as the night,
with two white stripes —
one near her head,
one near her tail.

Her face was purest gold, with big bright
eyes and a mouth shaped like a kiss.
The small fat body made the Clownfish look
like something good to eat,
especially to big, hungry fishes.

The Clownfish was very small.
She could very easily be gobbled up by a
big, hungry fish.
Now,
how could the Clownfish keep from being eaten?
Was there any way this small creature
could solve this problem?
Why yes, there was.
The Clownfish began a friendship with the
Anemone.
She swam a "getting-to-know-you" dance
around the Anemone —
up and down and way around,
up and down and way around,
closer and closer.
The little Clownfish curved to brush gently
against the Anemone's stinging tentacles —
time and again,
time and again.

Drawings by Arabelle Wheatley

It was a lovely dance.
At first the Anemone stung the Clownfish,
but she kept on brushing gently
against the tentacles for almost an hour.
Slowly the Anemone came to know the Clownfish.
Finally the tentacles stopped stinging, and
the Anemone made the Clownfish welcome.
The small black fish with white stripes and
golden face nestled safely
among the Anemone's tentacles.
The two were partners
for the rest of their lives.
The other anemones and clownfish on the reef
found partners the same way.

One day a great big fish came looking
for a meal.
It saw the little Clownfish.
With mouth wide open, the big fish darted
toward the Clownfish.
The Clownfish swam straight to the Anemone
and hid among the tentacles.
The Anemone stung the big fish very hard
and drove it away.

Hiding from big hungry fish wasn't such a
problem now for the Clownfish.
And the Clownfish helped the Anemone get
extra food to eat.
Sometimes she found bits of drifting food
and took them back to the Anemone:
one piece for the Anemone,
one piece for the Clownfish;
one for you,
one for me.
It was a fine partnership.
One day, instead of food,
the Clownfish brought home a surprise.
Another clownfish—a male.
The little female had found a mate.
She was ready to raise a family.
After getting to know each other, the
Anemone welcomed the male clownfish.
Both clownfish were safe from their enemies.
And their eggs would be too.

That is how three small sea creatures
on a coral reef in a warm and sunny sea,
made life easier —
just by helping each other.

MARK HAS A FIELD DAY

by Carsten Ahrens

Drawings by Les Gray

Mark Howe came downstairs to a farm breakfast after a night filled with dreams of his winning the 7th-8th grade race at the Fourth of July picnic. He had come in second last year. This year he had practiced for the last six weeks to better his chances of winning.

But his father had other plans. "Mark," he said, "our thirty rows of potatoes are crawling with potato beetles. I'm giving up my Fourth of July holiday to work with Al White on the pasture fence. You'll have to get at those beetles and kill them. We need to have a good harvest. I'm sorry, Mark."

Mark's appetite for breakfast was gone. He followed his father and picked up a pail that was partly filled with kerosene. His father handed him a paddle.

Out in the field Mark placed the pail under a potato plant. Then he tapped the stalks gently with the paddle. The insects played "possum," dropped from the leaves, and fell to their death in kerosene.

His mother tried to cheer him up. "Mark," she called, "you'll be through before the races begin."

Mark and his father looked at each other and shook their heads. They knew better: The job would take all day. Ned Stark would win the race again this year!

Before him was the big potato field, green with healthy leaves and white with flowers. Mark was terribly discouraged. He sat down suddenly and though he shut his eyes tightly, tears squeezed through. He waited a moment and when he looked up, his self-pity changed to anger. Stalking through an open gate at the far end of the field was neighbor Burton's flock of turkeys. Mark knew he'd have to take more time to drive those two hundred birds home!

Full of fury, Mark dashed toward the turkeys. But it was a big field and before he reached them, he stopped in amazement. The great birds were eating the potato beetles! They paid no attention to Mark as they ate the tender, young pink beetles as well as the old ones that had hard, striped shells. The turkeys stuck out their heads on long, flexible necks and examined each plant so they wouldn't miss a single bug.

"Those turkeys might be just what I need," Mark muttered. "I don't think I'll chase them out right away."

He got behind the flock and slowly drove the birds down the rows of plants. The potato field was equally divided by a drainage ditch with fifteen rows on either side. Mark herded the turkeys evenly over the east side and then let them move at their own speed. They made rustling noises as their eyes and beaks, hidden in the potato branches, hunted food.

When the lower end of the field was reached, Mark carefully steered the flock around and started up the final fifteen rows. Then disaster! Rags, Mark's spaniel, came zigzagging across the field yipping and yapping after a rabbit. Both were headed for the center of the flock of turkeys.

Mark got a big clod of dirt and threw it at the pair. It exploded in the air and came down all over them. The rabbit, then Rags, suddenly turned to the left and missed the flock. Soon Rags's yapping came from a long way off.

As the turkeys neared the end of the field, Mark was afraid the birds would be filled up. He had to work harder to keep them on the job. Many turkeys tried to turn from the potato plants but Mark kept urging them along the green rows.

Finally the bugs were eaten off the last plant. Mark had nothing but love for the turkeys. They had saved him hours of work. They looked funny, for their crammed crops made them look lopsided and top-heavy. The impossible job was done, well done.

Mrs. Burton came to meet him as he drove the turkeys homeward. "I'm sorry our turkeys got out, Mark," she said.

"Don't apologize," Mark said, laughing. "Your turkeys helped me kill a bumper crop of potato beetles!"

Rags came back panting from the rabbit chase, and he and Mark trotted down the lane. They passed the beetle-free potato field. The turkeys had saved the day. It was still an hour before the races, and Ned Stark might not win. Mark began to whistle.

by Thorn Bacon

No one really knows why Hubert, a gentle, three-ton hippopotamus, decided to take a 1000-mile stroll across South Africa some thirty years ago. Nor can anyone who remembers Hubert explain the huge rain cloud that rumbled in the sky above him everywhere he went.

But Hubert's strange journey is a fact. It is also true that his rain cloud sprinkled the land with life-giving water at a time when the crops were withering from heat, and wild animals were going hungry because the grass had dried up and was blowing away.

Zulu tribesmen who first saw Hubert said he sloshed out of a Swaziland swamp in answer to their prayers for rain. His rain cloud was a gift from the Umpundulo bird, which the Zulus believe makes lightning and thunder by beating its bright wings together. They said Hubert saved the magical bird from a hungry crocodile. In return the Umpundulo gave the hippo a rain cloud which he could turn on and off to keep his skin wet should he ever decide to leave his river home for any reason.

"Nonsense," scoffed the white Boer farmers of South Africa. "Hubert was a hippo

63

Drawings by Gordon Kibbee

who had been driven away from his herd after losing a fight over his sweetheart to an older hippo. As for the rain cloud, that was just chance. It was time for a change in the weather anyway."

Hubert first drew official notice in Eshowe, South Africa, when Civil Commissioner John Robertson was awakened by a telephone call from the chief of police.

"Hate to disturb you so early in the morning, old boy," the chief said, "but there's a hippo barging through the streets. He seems harmless enough, but I guess something ought to be done about him."

The protection of wild animals was part of Robertson's duties as civil commissioner, so he dressed quickly and rushed out of his house, only

to run back in again to get his umbrella. It was raining for the first time in months!

When Robertson reached his office, there indeed was Hubert munching happily on some large rubber plant leaves in the commissioner's garden. Hubert was a large bull, with gleaming ivory tusks. He had bulging red-rimmed eyes and a hide with long battle scars.

Though he knew hippos are gentle by nature, Robertson also knew they have short tempers if alarmed. But he was worried about his garden. It would fit nicely into Hubert's ten-foot stomach with room to spare.

Robertson gave Hubert a cautious poke with his umbrella. "Shoo!" he said, "you're trespassing on government property."

With a gusty sigh Hubert started down the street. Robertson kept an eye on him for several hours and noticed that the dripping rain cloud in the sky drifted slowly south. It seemed to stay right over Hubert until he reached the edge of town. The hippo stopped only twice before he left Eshowe. He inspected a fruit stand and paused to look at a poster of Elvis Presley in front of a movie theater.

That night in the tall Sen grass just outside town, Zulu tribesmen danced thanks around Hubert for bringing them rain. Hubert, however, snored through the ceremony.

The next morning Robertson sent telegrams to all of his game wardens: "Protect harmless hippo on tour. Natives think he is a rain god."

In the months following his visit to Eshowe, Hubert turned up at Hindu temples, browsed in Bantu cabbage patches and sniffed at automobiles and rickshaws. He got into serious trouble only once when he started eating his way through a sugarcane field. The angry farmer who owned the field was persuaded not to shoot Hubert by some citizens who passed the hat to pay for the damage. Then they cheered the hippo on his way.

By the time Hubert had swum the Pongola River and was heading toward the large city of Durban between rain showers he had become famous. Along the highway crowds of people cheered him and put out cabbages, hay, sugarcane and rubber plant leaves for him to eat. The Durban newspapers praised Hubert, saying that it didn't matter whether or not he was a rain god. He had brought showers with him wherever he traveled. Wasn't this proof enough that he was special?

Not everybody believed Hubert was extraordinary. Zoologists said hippos do not have to take a river bath every day and that Hubert was no exception. He only had to have lots of water to drink. Therefore there was nothing terribly unusual about Hubert's 700-mile journey. He was simply a smart hippo who had sense

enough to get in under the rain. The rain cloud wasn't following Hubert; Hubert was following the rain cloud.

Nevertheless, on the day Hubert reached Durban, hundreds of people waited to greet him beside a huge "Welcome Hubert" sign. The mayor made a speech. Then he and a police escort led the wandering hippo to a real hero's welcome at Victoria

Park, where thousands of people waited.

Later in the day, Hubert left Durban going toward the town of Komgha. It was about 300 miles away, or a year's walk for a hippo.

There, a whole year later, a strange thing happened: It stopped raining and Hubert disappeared. Angry citizens at first thought he had been kidnapped for a zoo in another city. Later a dead hippo was found in a sugarcane field. It was believed to be Hubert.

The Zulus had a different story. Hubert was a rain god who answered their prayers for an end to the drought. After traveling for almost three years, he grew tired, met a lady hippopotamus and made a home among the water lilies of some quiet river.

The Zulus believe he will come back if they ever badly need rain again. Many South Africans believe to this day that the Zulus were right about Hubert.

Meadow Mystery

by Beverly Letchworth

Come into my meadow. Pretty, isn't it? See the Queen Anne's lace, the red and white clover, the timothy hay? The yellow hawkweed is blooming too.

What, you don't know who I am? Or where I am? You're not supposed to. If you could find me right off, it would mean I'm not very well hidden.

There is danger in my meadow, you know. Many little creatures are eaten by bigger ones. I can't be too careful. See the wasps buzzing around? They are really my enemies.

I could tell you who I am, but wouldn't you like to guess first? No, I'm not the toad sitting under the strawberry plant. And I'm not the white-footed mouse hiding in the grass. I've already given you some clues.

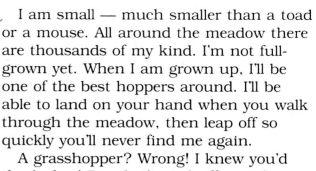

Drawings by Peter Zallinger

I am small — much smaller than a toad or a mouse. All around the meadow there are thousands of my kind. I'm not full-grown yet. When I am grown up, I'll be one of the best hoppers around. I'll be able to land on your hand when you walk through the meadow, then leap off so quickly you'll never find me again.

A grasshopper? Wrong! I knew you'd think that! But don't get huffy. You're on the right track. I am an insect, but not a grasshopper.

You say you still can't see me? Well, I'm hiding. Look closely at the red clover plants around you. What do you see?

Well, I have to give you more credit. You're right. You see a little blob of white foam. That's my shelter. I built it. Isn't it grand? I hide in here. It does protect me from the sun and keeps me nice and moist, too.

Do you see me inside? Of course not! Take a plant stem and try to find me. Yes, the bubbly stuff is sticky. It helps my shelter hold its shape. You see, I stay on plants and suck the juices from them. Most of this sap passes right through me and comes out my tail end as a special liquid called honeydew. Then I blow air into the honeydew until it becomes a bubbly foam.

I can feel you poking around, but you haven't found me yet. Isn't my foam great protection? If you were a wasp flying over me right now, you wouldn't be able to see me through the thick foam. Even if a wasp did strike, chances are it would miss, because I would have skittered to another part of my shelter.

Okay, I'll stop moving now so you can find me. Careful, now. Let me crawl out on the stem.

Yes, there are lots of us spittlebugs here in the meadow.

I'm afraid you're right. Sometimes we spittlebugs *do* cause trouble in gardens, orchards or hayfields. Sometimes we hurt the plants we are feeding on. But usually we are just a small part of the meadow community.

Well, it's been nice meeting you. You've been very gentle and kind with me. And you were patient with my little game of *guess who*.

If you'll excuse me now, I would like to finish my dinner. Come back in a few weeks when I'm grown, and I may jump on your hand as you walk by. Or maybe another spittlebug will find you. With a little luck and a sharp eye, you may get to know many of us.

There are enemies all around, so I must hurry and make my bubble shelter ▲ . Later I'll crawl out as an adult ◄ and hop about the meadow. Maybe I'll hop on you!

I guess I'm not much to look at — just a yellow insect, only as long as a grain of rice. Didn't my bubbly home give you a clue? I'm a *spittlebug!* Some people call me a *froghopper*.

Right now I'm still growing. I am a *nymph*. As an adult I'll be bigger and have wings. Then I'll leave my foam shelter to hop around the meadow.

In the fall we spittlebugs lay eggs that won't hatch until spring, when a new crop of spittlebug nymphs arrives. Next summer there will be more bubbly homes all around the meadow.

Please put me back now. I feel very uneasy out in the open. In just a minute I'll be buried deep in my foam again. Do you see some of the other homes of my neighbors? Look on the clover plants.

by Beth Wagner

"All right, Sandy, all the way up and over!" shouted the trainer. Sandy, a California sea lion, was swimming full speed underwater and couldn't hear a word. But she knew what to do. Sandy leaped from the shallow pool and smoothly sailed over the bar the trainer was holding. Then she did a backflip, slipped out of the water, and slid all the way to her box. The crowd applauded loudly.

"*Aaaarrrrgggg,*" bellowed the sea lion star. Swaying back and forth on her perch, Sandy waited for her reward. Sometimes it was a pat on the head; this time it was a piece of fish. With one gulp, she swallowed it whole. Then Tom, the trainer, turned to end the show. Swiftly, Sandy poked her nose into the open fish container hanging on his belt. Sandy pretended to gulp down a few more bits before Tom caught her.

"Now, Sandy, behave your——" but she stopped him by leaning forward on her belly, clapping her flippers together, and barking all at once. The audience laughed and cheered. It looked as though Sandy were stealing food from Tom, but it was really just part of the show. Sandy raised a flipper to the crowd and the show was over.

Now it was time for the star performer to rest. Tom quickly guided Sandy to her pool area. There she joined the other sea lions on a flat ledge surrounded by jagged rocks.

Only three years ago, Sandy had been born near rocks much like the ones around her now. But her birth had taken place in the wild—on a lonely island near the California coast.

At that time Sandy and the other sea lions spent much of their time lying in the sun and sleeping. They also liked to play in the water. Sometimes they wrestled and chased each other. At other times they went body-surfing, popping in and out of the waves.

SANDY SEA LION

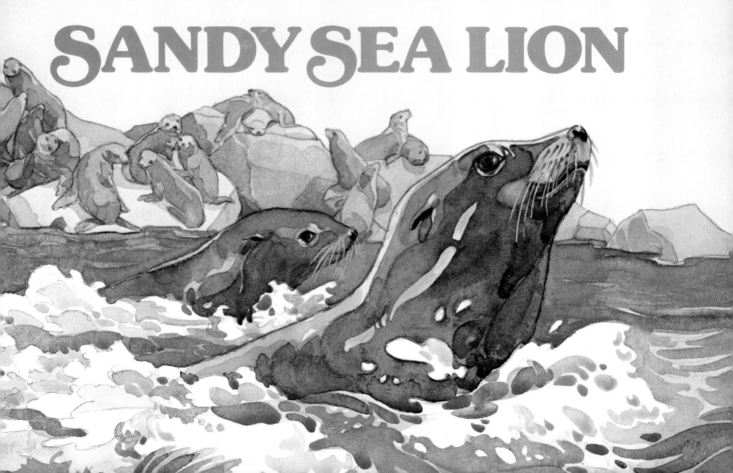

Drawings by Renée Quintal Daily

One afternoon when Sandy was a year old, she dived into the water near the coast with some other sea lion pups from her colony. The others played tag and barked loudly in their excitement. But Sandy swam slowly by herself.

After the game, the group headed back to their island. Sandy, though, was too weak to swim with the other pups. She had eaten fish that had worms in them. Now these small worms were living in her lungs. Because of these worms, her lungs could not take in enough air.

It was so hard for Sandy to breathe that she rode a wave in to shore. Then she beached herself above the high tide line. Out of the water, she could rest and breathe more easily.

"What's the matter with that poor sea lion?" people asked each other as they gathered quickly around Sandy.

Fortunately, a lifeguard understood what had happened. "Sometimes seals, whales, and other marine mammals beach themselves because they're sick," she explained to the crowd.

"Can we take the sea lion home?" a small boy asked his mother. "I'll bet I could fix him."

"It's nice of you to want to help," the lifeguard said. "But you have to have a special permit to take animals from the beach."

The boy frowned. Then the lifeguard added, "Don't worry about this animal, though. I'll call the rescue team at Sea World. They have a permit to remove sick animals. And they'll try to help the sea lion get well."

When Sandy first arrived at Sea World, she was put in an area by herself. The keepers knew that the best way to cure Sandy was to give her plenty of rest. They also knew that her food had to be free of any new worms. One by one, the worms already in Sandy's lungs would grow old and die.

The keepers' plan worked! Sandy's lungs began to heal. At the end of six months, Sandy joined the other healthy sea lions at Sea World. But she would never be able to go free. There was no way to completely repair the parts of her lungs that had been damaged. Sandy could swim in shallow water, but she couldn't dive deep to get food.

One day, a piece of wood drifted into the pool where Sandy was swimming. She picked the wood up and tossed it around the pool by herself. Then she played "catch" with another sea lion.

While Sandy was playing, Tom Batchelor, an animal trainer, watched her carefully. He wanted another sea lion for the shows Sea World put on each afternoon. Pointing to Sandy, he said to the other trainers, "She looks like a good one. We'll start training her tomorrow."

Training went well for Sandy. Whenever she learned a new trick, Tom rewarded her with petting, toys, play time with other sea lions, or food.

Sandy's love of attention was only one of the reasons she was so easy to train. She was also very curious and she learned quickly—a perfect combination!

At first, Sandy learned the easy stunts: slapping her flippers together, and sliding up to a sitting position on a large box. Before long she was doing high dives and turning somersaults down the length of the pool.

Sandy seemed to like her new home. There were no enemies, and she had the other sea lions to keep her company.

But showtime was the best part of each day for Sandy. After each trick, Tom gave her a reward. And the happy people around her clapped wildly. After all, Sandy was the star of the show!

SNOWBEARS

Drawings by Linda K. Powell

by Helen Evetts

A tiny cloud of breath rose from a big snowdrift. That was the only sign that a creature was living in the mother polar bear's winter home on the Siberian tundra.

Inside the den two newborn cubs — blind and nearly naked — were snuggled in their mother's thick, warm underfur. They were small and pink, only about the size of a full-grown guinea pig. And they couldn't yet move about on their own.

Mother Bear lay back against the den wall, holding Alexei and Petya on her body. There she suckled them and kept them warm. Even though it was much warmer inside than out, they would have frozen on the icy floor of their cavern.

Polar bears' milk is very rich; it's as thick as canned condensed milk. Drinking it, the twins grew very fast and soon were fat little "snowballs." Their first, fine short hair grew longer and coarser and kept them warm. Their small, blunt ears were soon covered with woolly hair. When they were about a month old they were struggling to crawl about the den, and their eyes were beginning to open.

At three months Alexei and Petya could see, hear and smell. They measured 24 inches (61 cm) from their shiny black button noses to the tips of their stubby tails. They weighed about 20 pounds (9 kg) each. By now they were romping all over their patient mother.

On a still March day, Mother Bear started to break out of the den. To get out, she had to knock down the frozen den wall. She pushed against it with her heavy body. She scratched at the ice with her strong, curving claws. At last she burst out into the sunlight. The bright light startled the cubs, and they didn't want to follow her. They cowered at the

the ice shelf over the ocean there would be seals, the snowbear's staple food. But on the cubs' first day out of the den, she had to make do with what she could find. The cubs were too small to travel fast and too new to the Arctic world for her to leave them for long.

For many days they did not go far. Mother Bear kept feeding milk to the growing cubs but grew hungrier and hungrier herself. She was lucky when she found a piece of dead seal which another bear had left behind. Each night the bears returned to their snow den.

One day the three polar bears traveled far enough to reach the ice over the ocean. Mother Bear was now terribly hungry. She was a skilled hunter, but hunting seals also meant a long wait.

First she had to find a breathing hole which a seal had made through the ice from the water underneath. Though the

back of the den, blinking. Mother Bear came back, picked them up in her mouth and carried them out.

The twins were still very small and delicate to brave the fierce Arctic cold. As Mother Bear headed for the shoreline, she made many stops to warm and feed her babies.

Grubbing under the snow, she found some food for herself — lichens, grasses and berries. For five months she had lived on her body fat in the den. She now needed more to eat than the plant leftovers from nature's deep freeze. Out on hole was covered with a mound of snow, her keen nose smelled seal. Now it was time to hide her cubs in a snowbank. Then she scraped the snow from the seal's hole to begin her wait. Seals poke up their heads to breathe every few minutes. They use several different breathing holes. Today she was lucky. She didn't have to wait long before a seal's nose popped up. With one smack of her huge forepaw, she killed it.

Mother Bear could hardly wait to claw open the hole to drag the heavy seal onto the ice. She was hungry enough to eat almost all of the 150 pounds (68 kg) of seal. But some of the blubber she dragged to the cubs' hiding place to let them have a few bites. Then it was time to amble back to their den, the mother's head swaying from side to side on her thick neck.

As they grew, the cubs tried to do everything their mother did. Alexei and Petya learned to slide down snow slopes on their fat bellies, short legs spread wide. They learned to "freeze," or lie still, behind a snow mound when Mother Bear pushed them down. If they ran after her, she cuffed them with her heavy paw and sent them back into hiding.

Soon the polar bear family no longer returned to the den to sleep.

All summer they stayed out on the ice. To the twin cubs the Arctic world was a playground; to Mother Bear it was a place of many dangers. She was always on the lookout for predators. She wasn't afraid for herself or for the cubs when she was with them. She could drive off any male polar bear hungry enough to eat her cubs. But when their mother wasn't around, then Petya and Alexei were defenseless. So when she left them to find food for herself, she hid them. The polar bears' winter fur — almost as white as the snow — blended with the surroundings. In summer it was more creamy yellow like the old sea ice when it broke up.

One day Mother Bear was away longer than usual. Alexei bit Petya's ear and a fight started. Petya bit back, snarling with rage. The two of them rolled over and over, biting, scratching and snarling.

If the cubs had kept quiet, Old Igor, a huge male polar bear, might not have seen them. Old Igor weighed about 900 pounds (405 kg) and was 9 feet (3 m) long. He had just missed a seal lying on the ice. It flipped into the water before he could grab it and looked up at him from the water. Old Igor turned in anger. Then he saw the cubs fighting! Quietly, on his fur-soled feet, he stalked them.

That day Mother Bear had not traveled far. She had found the remains of a dead whale that she had smelled on the wind. She ate all she could. When loping back to her cubs, she caught Old Igor's strong scent. The coarse hair on her neck and shoulders bristled. She charged at him to rescue her cubs. Though she weighed about 200 pounds (90 kg) less than Old Igor, he turned tail and ran.

It would be many months and another winter-denning with Mother Bear before the cubs could care for themselves. They still had to grow much bigger and learn to hunt seals.

Rangers: Polar bears live all around the Arctic—along the coasts of Norway and the length of the USSR to the Bering Straits, also from northern Alaska to northern Labrador, and in Greenland and Spitsbergen. There are none living wild in the southern hemisphere.

Full-grown polar bears have few predators. Humans are their only deadly enemies, but the bears don't seem greatly afraid of people. In the USSR polar bears are strictly protected. When some happen to wander into the research stations, they are chased away with flares and noise. The Soviet Union, the United States, Norway, Denmark and Canada have signed an international agreement to study and conserve polar bears.

R.R.

White-footed
mouse

Weasel

Bird's nest

gussie goes hunting

by Mary Mastin

Gussie was a garter snake. She was very pretty with her bright black eyes and three lemon-yellow stripes. One stripe ran straight down the center of her back. The same kind of bright line went down each of her sides to the tip of her tail, twenty-four inches from her head. In between the stripes, Gussie was dark and spotted.

Gussie
the garter snake

She must also have been a sensible snai for she knew exactly what to do when spri began to warm the countryside. She crawl slowly out of her winter den in the old ro pile and stretched out on her favorite lc Most of her days were spent dozing in the su and at night she went back to the rock pile

After two weeks of slowly waking up, Guss went to look for food and a summer hom She slid over the tree roots and through t dry leaves with only the slightest rustlir sound. She was hunting for a fat little mous but they all seemed to be hiding where Guss couldn't find them.

On she went to the edge of the woods ar out into a small meadow. Softly she mov through the new grass, her forked tongue da ing out ahead. She used it to feel her way ar pick up the scent of food. As she pulled h tongue back, and touched the roof of h mouth with it, she caught a familiar sme Only a few feet away was a thick clump

Black
snake

Mink

eds and low bushes. Silently she slipped
rough the rough stalks. She had found a
rd's nest with eggs in it!

She pushed her face up over the nest's edge
. right into another face. Gussie hissed a
rning. Too late, she saw the sharply pointed
se and wicked little eyes of a weasel—one
her deadliest enemies. What a mistake! She
cked away so quickly that she looped over
r own tail, nearly turning herself upside
wn. No eggs for breakfast this morning!

The narrowness of her escape sent her
eaking across the meadow, to hide in the
eds along the edge of the river.

Soon her quick eyes saw the top of a blunt
se coming toward her. She tensed, ready to
atch the frog headfirst in her mouth. But it
sn't a frog; it was a big bad-tempered old
ack snake with a huge appetite for young
rter snakes. She turned tail and fled. She

shot over a rock and under an old pine stump
beside the river. She slid into a small hole
and was stopped by a pair of fiery eyes and
a mouthful of snarling teeth that belonged to
an unfriendly mink!

Whsst! Gussie backed out of the burrow
and turned. Scrunch! The teeth closed on her
tail. She tried to wriggle up over the stump, but
one of the roots broke, sending her and the
mink into the river.

Gussie was free, but still frightened.

She swam swiftly upstream until she came
to a small sandy bay. Now tired, she began to
float toward the shore. Suddenly she found
herself in the middle of a school of minnows.
They were so scared and confused they swam
right into her mouth.

After gobbling her breakfast, Gussie
wriggled up on the beach to safety under a
large boulder.

Any sensible snake would spend the summer there and that was just what Gussie did!

Leopard
frog

Drawing by Darrell Wiskur

Minnows

77

Why did that little spring
Come tumbling out here?
Was it tired of underground
Where things are dark and drear?

Did it yearn for sunlight
To glow upon its face?
Did it hear of mossy beds
And Queen Anne's lace?

Or did it know a child lives
Where this maple grows
Who needed such a little spring
For dabbling his toes?

—Solveig Paulson Russell

Cathy Creek

by Richard Rainey

One day last summer, a couple of weeks after school was out, I was mowing our front lawn. I had almost finished when I discovered a patch of wet grass where the ground was soft and spongy. Every time I mowed it I left footprints and tire tracks behind. The wet patch was shaped like a football and was about twice as long as my bike. It seemed kind of a funny thing to happen to the lawn.

That night, just at dusk, I was out watching bats and swallows catching bugs when my neighbor, Cathy, came over. I showed her the wet patch. She said she thought it was a spring. I did too.

The following week when it was time to mow the lawn again, the grass in the wet patch was a lot taller than the rest of the yard. The ground was so soft the mower just sank in. Instead of being able to mow straight across it I had to mow in-and-out from the edges. I couldn't reach the grass in the middle.

By the Fourth of July the wet part of our lawn was really something. It had a bubbling spring in it and a swampy area about 30 feet long. Bunches of grass stuck straight up in the middle of it. Water flowed from the "swamp" making a big puddle on the lower end of the driveway near a forsythia bush.

Birds began to bathe in the driveway puddle. The water was pretty cold where it bubbled up out of the lawn, but the sun warmed it where it crossed the driveway. That's where the birds took their baths! A pair of wrens with a nest in a maple tree just above the swamp were always splashing around. Sparrows came half a dozen at a time to drink and bathe. Robins came to drink and tug worms out of the mud around the swamp, but I never saw them bathe.

try to catch them. They would skim along the surface halfway upstream and then coast back. Gnats, mosquitoes and other tiny flying things got pretty thick, but at the same time spiders built webs among the forsythia leaves and caught hundreds of insects.

It was amazing. Where had all these plants and bugs come from? Before the spring bubbled up, I had seen none living anywhere in the yard. Probably some plant seeds had been blown in on the wind, or else were carried in by birds. I can't remember whether birds got to our swamp and stream first, or whether I saw plants first.

Drawings by Richard Cuffari

Dad said that the water from the puddle was makir the end of the driveway ca in. So at the end of summe just before school began, h had me take the hoe and scrape a trench from the p dle down into the backyard The water flowed out of th puddle about 30 or 40 feet a disappeared into the groun

When the puddle was go the water skaters, gnats an plants disappeared. In the puddle's place I had a long thin stream. It was about 1 feet long, including the swar

In autumn the leaves fel into the swamp and mixed with the mud. They were ha

Cathy spent a lot of time watching the birds *and* trying to keep our Siamese cat away from them.

After a while the strangest things began to grow in the water. There were long gray stalks like pieces of fuzzy string and there was a leaf that looked like fern, except it was brown instead of green. Near where the water flowed in, a yellowish scum grew on the surface of the puddle.

Water bugs also lived in the puddle. They were the kind that skate on the surface and move like lightning when you

80

to rake out, so finally I just left them. The leaves packed down and after a while less mud washed onto the driveway. The leaves made a smooth bed for the water to flow over.

During the winter the swamp was like a garden. There the grass stayed green and fresh-looking. It was never covered with snow, even when enough fell to close our school. On cold sunny days it was nice to see sparkling water flowing through the stretch of bright green grass. Often small clouds of steam rose above it.

Winter did magical things to the new section of stream I had dug. All winter water flowed through it. It pushed sand and gravel along and made my trench deeper. While the water was digging down into the earth, the frozen ground on both sides lifted up.

When spring came I could see that a stream bed had been made. It was only about 12 inches wide and maybe 3 inches deep, but it was the real thing! I looked closely and saw tiny snails crawling on the dead leaves. When I turned one of the leaves over, the water came to life! Round red specks the size of pin-heads scurried for cover. Shrimplike creatures darted wildly about before disappearing beneath another leaf.

The night I went out with a flashlight I knew for sure we had a real stream. I saw a pink salamander hunting for insects at the water's edge.

Not many people have a chance to see a stream get started. It's fun watching a wet place on the lawn grow into a *real* stream. Our stream is about 100 feet long now and I think I'll name it "Cathy Creek."

TARRED FEATHERS

by Vivian Vernon

"Stop the tractor, Dad!" Dale yelled above the roar of the tractor's motor and the clatter of the corn planter they were hauling down the road.

Mr. Porter figured something must be wrong, so he stopped on the shoulder of the road. Dale jumped off and raced up the road.

"What's wrong?" his dad called after him.

"They're stuck! Back at the crossroad! We've got to help them!" Dale yelled over his shoulder.

"Who's stuck? Shall I bring the tractor?" Mr. Porter shouted.

"No, I'll get them. They're baby bobwhite quail," Dale puffed.

"You poor little things," Dale said as he reached the intersection. He swung his long legs over the barricade that had been placed there to keep cars off the freshly tarred road.

The road seemed full of loudly peeping baby quail. Their newly feathered wings were beating rapidly as they tried to free their feet, which were stuck in the gooey tar. The mother quail fluttered back and forth between the babies and the bushes, trying to coax the little ones to follow her.

Dale pulled off his battered hat. He lined the hat with his red kerchief and set it against a rock. By the time his dad reached the barricade, Dale had rolled up the legs of his blue jeans.

"Is it okay if I wear my sneakers in the tar, Dad?" he asked. "They're my old ones." Without waiting for an answer he stepped onto the gooey, sticky tar. The smell almost choked him. He gently pried the tiny quail feet loose, and one by one handed the trembling birds to his dad.

"What are you going to do with them?" his dad asked.

"Take them home and clean them up."

"What then?"

"Bring them back here to their mother, of course."

"How're you going to get the tar off their feet and wing feathers?"

"Don't you know?" Dale asked, surprised that his dad didn't have the answer.

"Sorry, this is my first experience at a tar-and-feather party," his dad joked.

"We could wash them in gasoline," Dale suggested hopefully.

"Their skin is too tender. Gas would burn them," answered Mr. Porter.

"Will detergent take it off?" asked Dale.

"Don't think so, but we can try," his dad said as he put the last of the thirteen baby quail in Dale's hat.

"It looks as if you left a sticky memorial to your rescue mission," he laughed as Dale pulled his own feet free of the clinging tar and left a pattern of tracks behind.

"Boy, wait'll Mom sees these," Dale said, cleaning his sticky shoes on a clump of grass.

"She'll be so excited over the quail she won't even see your shoes," his dad assured him.

"I'll bet Mr. Corey, the conservation agent, can tell me how to get the tar off these birds," Dale said as he cradled the hatful of chicks in his arms and started for the tractor.

"Good idea. That's using your head," Mr. Porter said approvingly. Then, noticing the mother quail, he added, "We're leaving an unhappy mother back there, Dale."

Drawings by John Mecray

"Look, Dad," Dale said, "She's limping and dragging her wing as if she's trying to get us away from her babies. She doesn't know they'll die unless we save them."

"At least we *hope* we can save them," his dad said cautiously.

"Let's hurry so we can get them back before she leaves," Dale suggested. And he ran to the tractor.

Dale held the hatful of birds in his arms as they clattered down the road. When they drove into the barnyard, he could see his mother sitting in the porch swing. He jumped off the tractor, kicked off his sneakers and dashed onto the porch.

"Here, Mom, hold these. I have to call Mr. Corey," and he plopped the hat in her lap.

"Baby quail!" she exclaimed, looking excitedly at the messy hatful of squirming, chirping chicks.

"They got caught in the fresh tar on that road by the intersection. I've got to find out how to clean them, fast," Dale said as the screen door slammed behind him.

Mr. Corey's voice over the phone was reassuring: "Try some vegetable oil," he said. "That should take the tar off. If it doesn't, let me know."

"Okay, thanks a lot, Mr. Corey," Dale said. He ran into the kitchen shouting, "Hey, Mom, please bring in the birds. Mr. Corey says vegetable oil will clean them!"

Dale spread newspapers on the floor and filled a bowl with vegetable oil. "Mr. Corey was right. It works," he said, washing the quails one by one. His mother rubbed them gently with an old towel and put them in a grocery carton.

By the time they finished, a pink and purple sunset was beginning to color the sky. Mrs. Porter drove Dale and the birds to the barricade.

"She's still there, Mom," Dale said happily when he saw the mother quail whisk into the bushes. He lifted the grocery carton from the back seat and carefully tipped it on its side in the grass. Thirteen little chicks squirmed and pushed over one another and fluttered their tar-free wings as they ran to their mother. Several of them went to the edge of the roadbed, then ran after the others into the bushes.

"Looks like they've learned their lesson," Dale laughed.

Mrs. Porter glanced at her watch. "And you've missed your Scout meeting," she reminded him.

"I've missed the meeting, but I've done thirteen good deeds today." Dale grinned as he plopped onto the car seat. "That's a record for me!"

WONDERS OF THE WILD:

the fennec

by Robert F. Gray

Zerda the fennec (FEN-nick) stays alive by using his wits and powerful legs. This tiny fox lives in the hot lands of North Africa. In the daytime he sleeps safely in his burrow, coiled into a fluffy, sand-colored ball. Then at sundown he awakens—hungry and thirsty—and scurries to the burrow's entrance.

One night Zerda carefully sniffed the air for danger. He studied each bush and listened for enemies with his four-inch-long ears. (They seemed much too large for an animal only about 18 inches long.) Satisfied that he was safe, he darted to a water hole where other fennecs were drinking.

After satisfying his thirst Zerda began to hunt, trotting briskly along the desert's hollows and ravines, nose to the ground, ears alert. Suddenly a skink (lizard) darted in front of him. Zerda leaped for it and, after a short chase, caught the lizard. He ate it and also two large beetles. Then he went into an orchard to eat figs that had fallen from the trees. Finally, just before dawn, he caught a mouse. But because he was full he dug a hole in the sand, dropped the mouse into it, then replaced the sand with fast, sideward pats of his muzzle. That mouse would be good some other time.

Satisfied that his future meal was safe, the fox turned homeward. It was then that Aureus (AWR-ee-us) the jackal saw him. Aureus had not eaten for three nights, and at the sight of the tiny fox he set off in pursuit. In half a dozen leaps he caught and pinned

Zerda. The terrified fox rolled over in the sand, kicking and biting. He accidentally caught the jackal by his nose and Aureus jumped back suddenly. Zerda streaked away —twisting and backtracking—trying to lose the long-legged jackal. But the race was too uneven and Aureus slowly closed the gap between them.

It was then that the fox's powerful legs came to his aid. He suddenly stopped running and began to dig madly in the soft sand. His forelegs threw the sand aside so rapidly that he seemed to be diving into the earth. When Aureus reached the spot, Zerda was deep beneath the surface. The jackal tried to unearth him, but Zerda stayed well out of reach, and finally the jackal gave up in disgust and slunk away.

Zerda stayed quietly beneath the sand. Only after the sun rose did he dig cautiously to the surface and stick his pointed muzzle out of the sand. He smelled no danger. He poked his head out. He neither saw nor heard an enemy. So he wriggled from his hole and raced homeward. He scurried along the tunnels that connected his burrow with those of other fennecs. Reaching his own neat, grass-lined den, he flopped down, curled himself into a fluffy ball, and instantly fell asleep.

The fennec's scientific name is *Fennecus zerda*. The desert (or common) jackal's name is *Canis aureus*.

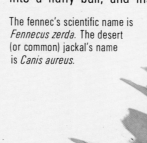

Drawing by
Margaret Estey

85

pelorus jack

by Lee Stowell Cullen

Drawing by John Mecray

There is a saying that man's best friend is his dog. But if I had my way, I would say man's best friend is the dolphin. In all the stories that have been written about these graceful, fun-loving creatures with their built-in grins, never once has it been recorded that a dolphin attacked a human. Instead, they are loving animals who seem to enjoy being around people.

As far back as the ancient Greeks and Romans, the dolphin has been known to help man. There are many stories that tell of ways in which dolphins have saved people's lives.

Because they are highly intelligent, dolphins have been trained by man to do many things. They have been taught all sorts of tricks to perform for us. They have also been trained by the United States Navy as valuable members of underwater study teams. The dolphins have been taught to carry messages and tools to human divers. They are trained to help rescue a diver in trouble.

Perhaps the most famous dolphin of all was "Pelorus Jack." About 85 years ago New Zealand sailors suddenly noticed that every time their ships started through the narrow, dangerous Cook Strait, an almost-white dolphin would appear near the side of the ship. It would leap and splash playfully in the water.

After a while the dolphin would move to the bow and swim from side to side just ahead of the ship. It seemed to be leading the vessel away from the dangerous shoals on either side of the strait. If two ships were headed through at one time, Pelorus Jack would flash ahead of the faster one and lead them both through.

**The famous white dolphin
watched and waited for the ships.
For twenty years he led them through
the dangerous channel.**

Pelorus Jack never turned away until the ship he was guiding was safely through the strait. Only then would he swim back, the same way he had come, to wait for the next ship. It didn't matter whether it was day or night, Pelorus Jack was there. Moving through the strait in the dark, he would leave a trail of sparkling water behind him. He never misjudged a ship's speed and he never got caught by the propellers.

To the people who watched him the dolphin became a good-luck charm. They thought that so long as he was there nothing bad would happen to their ship.

Before very long the passengers and crews of every ship going through the strait would line the decks to see their faithful friend. The sight of his sleek body slicing through the water meant a safe passage. The dolphin never let them down.

Pelorus Jack became so famous that the New Zealand government was concerned about the animal's safety. They passed a special law granting him lifelong protection. At that time it was unusual for a government to make laws to protect animals, especially a single animal.

Pelorus Jack didn't know this, of course. He just kept right on taking ships through Cook Strait, flipping his tail or leaping high in the air as passengers and crew applauded.

Then one day Pelorus Jack disappeared. For weeks people watched anxiously for him. He never appeared again. No one knows what happened to him. But for twenty years this wonderful dolphin, faithful and true to his friends, had led ship after ship out of danger into the safety of a calm harbor.

Screams and Whispers

by Judy Braus

Ryan hurried down the street in his lizard costume. Tonight was his nature club's Halloween party! He turned in at his friend Larry's house and knocked on the door.

"Hi, Ryan! Wow, you look great!" Larry exclaimed as he opened the door. "Just a second. I need to get some tin cans to go with my goat costume," said Larry, joking. "Tonight should be great for spooking! There's even supposed to be a full moon."

"I can't wait to see Mr. Elliott's costume. And Sue said she was coming as a jellyfish or a bat," said Ryan as he adjusted his mask.

"Boy, don't we make a great pair — a goat and a lizard," chuckled Larry. "You know, this will be the first time I've seen the old house Mr. Elliott bought."

"Same here," answered Ryan. "My sister said some people think his house is haunted. Some weird old lady used to live there and they say her ghost makes strange noises at night."

"Oh, Ryan, there are no such things as ghosts," said Larry as the boys started off down the street.

"Anyway, from now on all our nature club meetings will be at Mr. Elliott's. So maybe we'll get a chance to find out."

"The house is down this road," said Ryan, pointing. "It's getting dark . . . we'd better hurry."

When the boys got there, they knocked on the door, and Mr. Elliott opened it.

"*Eek!*" he screamed, pretending to be scared. Then he laughed. "Great costumes, boys! Come on in. We have lots to do before the rest of the gang gets here."

As Ryan and Larry stepped inside they heard a loud crash on the side of the house.

"What's that?" Ryan asked.

"Oh, it's just one of the shutters blowing in the wind. Since I've only been here a week, I still have a lot to fix up," answered Mr. Elliott.

Ryan and Larry took off their masks and looked around the old house. In the dim light they could see shabby old furniture and faded wallpaper that was cracked and peeling. The place really looked terrible!

"Wow, it *does* look haunted," whispered Ryan.

"Yeah," said Larry. "It's *spooky.*"

"Come on, you guys," said Mr. Elliott. "There are black and orange streamers and some pumpkin faces to put up. Here's the tape. I'm off to the store to get cider and some apples for bobbing."

As Mr. Elliott walked out, Ryan noticed the full moon shining outside.

"Look, Larry, it's a perfect night for vampires. There's the full moon."

"Not vampires, Ryan. It's werewolves that come out and howl when the moon is full."

"Come on, we've got to start decorating. Let's put the streamers here in the living room," said Ryan. "Hey — did you hear that?"

"Hear what?" asked Larry.

"That ticking sound," Ryan answered. "Shhh . . . listen."

Larry could just barely hear a slight *tick, tick, tick,* coming from the other side of the room.

"It's probably just an old clock," Larry said, shrugging his shoulders. He looked around. There was no clock in the room.

Then, just as suddenly as it had started, the ticking stopped.

Someone knocked on the door. Ryan ran to

open it. Standing on the porch was a huge vampire bat. Ryan gulped.

"Hi, Ryan," the bat said. "How do you like my costume? Neat, huh?"

"Is that you, Sue?" Ryan asked.

"Who did you think it was, silly?" laughed Sue, closing the door.

"Gosh, what a creepy house," said Sue, looking around.

"Ryan, Sue, come here — quick!" Larry called from the living room.

"What's wrong?" asked Ryan.

"Voices," whispered Larry. "Here, behind this wall. Listen."

"Oh, come on, Larry — voices?" laughed Sue. "How can people be talking behind a wall?"

Suddenly the ticking started again.

"What's that?" asked Sue. "It sounds kind of like a time bomb."

"We don't know what it is," said Ryan. "It keeps starting and stopping. Boy, this place is giving me the creeps."

"Aw, you guys, this is silly," said Sue.

"Maybe the old lady's ghost really *is* here," said Ryan with a shiver.

Just as he said that, the wind made a loud, moaning noise through a crack in a window. The kids moved closer to each other. Suddenly a scream filled the room. Everyone jumped.

"What was *that?*" whispered Ryan.

"It came from somewhere upstairs," Sue said.

"Let's see what's up there," said Larry.

"I wouldn't go up there if you paid me!" said Ryan. "Let's get out of here."

"Oh, it's probably just the wind," said Larry, hoping it was true.

"The *wind* doesn't scream, Larry," said Sue.

"Come on, let's just go see," urged Larry.

Suddenly another loud screech rang out.

"I'm getting out of here!" shouted Ryan. "This place really *is* haunted."

Larry and Sue were scared, too, but they stopped Ryan from leaving.

"Listen, let's get these decorations up and wait for Mr. Elliott," said Larry calmly. "He should be back any minute."

"Well," said Ryan, "OK, but let's all stick together until he gets here."

"So you really think the old lady is haunting this place?" asked Sue, hanging up a streamer.

"Who else would have screamed?" said Ryan.

Just then there was another scream. All three club members stopped what they were doing. Their hearts started beating faster.

"It's the old lady again," whispered Ryan. "Let's get out of here!" he added, heading for the door.

But just then Mr. Elliott walked in.

"What's going on?" he called.

"There are ghosts in here!" said Ryan, breathing quickly. "The old lady's screaming and, and, we're scared!"

"Tell him about the ticking," said Sue.

Mr. Elliott shook his head. "Wait a minute. Slow down and tell me what's happened."

"Well, we heard all these weird sounds: ticking but there's no clock, people whispering

be a hole to the outside so they can fly in and out. But in the winter, they stay huddled up together to keep warm. The noise is just their wings buzzing as they move back and forth.

"Now, let's go up to the attic and find the mysterious screamer," he said with a smile. "Let me get a flashlight."

They all followed Mr. Elliott up the creaky stairs. Mr. Elliott shined his light just as a huge owl flew out the broken attic window.

"It's a barn owl," he shouted, "and it's a beauty! That's your screamer, kids."

Larry looked at Ryan and Sue and started to laugh. "I guess we were pretty silly," he said with an embarrassed smile.

"Wait a minute. How about the ticking?" asked Ryan.

"Let's go find out," said Mr. Elliott.

When they were back in the living room, Larry pointed to an old rocking chair. "The ticking seemed to come from near that rocker."

Mr. Elliott looked around the chair. "See these piles of sawdust on the floor?" he asked. "I'll bet if you were to sit in that old rocker, it just might fall apart."

"How come?" asked Sue.

"Tiny insects called death-watch beetles are boring through the wood, and eating it. As they crawl, they make a ticking sound. It's just their hard outer covering knocking against the wood in the rocker."

He pulled off a piece of the rotting wood from the back of the chair. It was dry and crumbly.

"Look," he pointed. In his hand were a few tiny brown beetles. "Here they are!"

"And I thought those beetles were a clock!" said Ryan, laughing.

"Now do you still think my house is haunted?" asked Mr. Elliott.

"I just hope the owl, the beetles, and the bees trick the others when they get here! But let's not tell them, and see what happens," said Sue as she bit into a big red apple.

behind a wall, and just now screams upstairs," Ryan explained.

"Aren't you exaggerating?" Mr. Elliott smiled.

"Show him where the ticking and voices were, Larry," said Sue.

"Behind that wall," said Ryan, pointing.

Mr. Elliott leaned over and listened. The wallpaper had peeled away from the corner, and there was a crack in the wall. Mr. Elliott chuckled. "Do you remember what we talked about at our last club meeting?" he asked.

"Umm — honey bees," remembered Larry. "We were talking about how they survive the winter. But what does that have to do with us and this haunted house?"

"That's what's living in this wall. The bees have made their hive inside, and there must

BIG ED TALKS BACK

by Fred Johnson

On the way home from the store the other day, I stopped to watch the pigeons in the park. One big pigeon kept strutting back and forth in front of the bench where I sat. He seemed to be cocking a red eye at me, as if to stare at me suspiciously.

Soon the warm sun and pleasant breeze began to make me feel sleepy. My eyelids got heavier and heavier. My head began to droop — down, down, and ZZZZZZZ.

CHEEZ BITS

CHEEZ BIT

Drawings by Pidgeon

In a dream I thought I heard a gruff voice say, "*Cccccooooo,* hiya, bud! I'm Big Ed. Got any garbage with you?"

"What's this?" I said. "A talking pigeon! Is that really *you* talking?"

"It had better be," cooed Big Ed. "Do you see anyone else around here?"

"OK, it's fine with me if you want to talk, but why do you want garbage?" I asked.

"Because I'm bored with bread crumbs!" Big Ed replied. "That's all you people ever think of giving us — bread crumbs. You know, we pigeons like a change once in a while. We can peck a meal out of almost anything."

"That's for sure," I said. "Who says you guys are dumb? You know, I think it's exciting the way you pigeons can do tricks in the air and have races and carry messages."

Big Ed stuck his beak in the air and sneered, "Hold it! We're not *that* kind of pigeon. We're street pigeons — we make it on our own. Those fancy pigeons that people raise have to live in special coops and be fed special food. They're our sissy cousins. *We* survive almost anywhere. And those pigeons that carry messages aren't too bright anyway. They can only carry a message one way — from a distant place to their home coop. They can't take an answer back," he scoffed.

"Well, I've never seen them in action, but I've seen pigeons like you all my life. Where did you come from?" I asked.

Big Ed struck a pose, cleared his throat and began, "We have been around since long before civilization began. Our ancestors were wild rock doves from Europe and Asia. Some of them still live on the sides of cliffs there. Now *we* live on man-made cliffs," he explained.

"Man-made cliffs?" I asked.

"Of course. What do you think all those tall buildings are? Say, are you *sure* you don't have anything to eat with you?" he asked.

I remembered that I did have some cheese crackers in my grocery bag, so I told him about them.

"Well, hand 'em over," he demanded. "At least they're better than stale bread."

I got out the box, then crumbled a few crackers and tossed them on the ground. Three nearby pigeons fluttered over to help themselves. Big Ed threatened them with some *ccccoooos.* Then he drove them off with flapping wings and hard pecks.

"Gotta show 'em who's boss," he explained.

While he nibbled on the cheese cracker crumbs I asked him, "How do you live on our man-made cliffs?"

"They have windowsills, ledges, air conditioners, overhangs, gutters, roof corners. You name it, and we can roost on it or build a nest there," he answered.

I suddenly realized that I had never seen a pigeon nest, and said so.

Big Ed pecked at the last few cracker crumbs. He looked around cautiously, then came closer. "We build 'em where you can't get at 'em," he muttered out of the side of his beak. "There are a lot of you people who don't like us, you know."

"But in the city, where do you get enough grass to build your nests?" I wondered.

"Grass? Who needs it?" he cooed. "Sure, it comes in handy. But grass is for the birds. Give us a few sticks and some old rags or paper and we can pile up a fine nest."

"Well, your nests must work," I admitted. "There certainly are a lot of you around. You must raise *huge* families."

"Wrong!" he cooed loudly. "My mate lays only two eggs at a time. That's all."

"Then where do so many of you come from?" I asked.

With a careful look to make sure no one else was listening, Big Ed explained. "My mate lays only two eggs at a time, but she does it several times a year."

"Aha!" I said. "So that's it. Do baby pigeons eat bread crumbs and potato chips too?"

"Of course not," he replied. "For the first week after they hatch my mate feeds them a special 'pigeon milk' that we pigeons can make in our *crop.* That's a special food storage sac in our throat. Pigeon fathers make 'pigeon milk' too. So I can help feed the youngsters while she is laying eggs in another nest for her next brood."

"Then you have families at any time of year, I suppose."

"Almost. The winter months are not as good for family raising — but sometimes we try anyway. After all, there can't be too many of us. We have to stay ahead of all the people who try to get rid of us. Some even try to poison us!"

"Well, Ed," I said, "not all of us hate pigeons. You pigeons are pretty to watch as you flutter around in the sunlight. But you sure do make an ugly mess with your droppings. Can't you do anything about that?"

"Sorry; as long as there are pigeons there will be pigeon droppings. We certainly can't do anything about *that,*" he grumbled.

"No, I suppose you can't," I chuckled. "But your droppings can carry serious diseases. Pigeon droppings also eat away stone. Stone buildings and famous stone statues all over the world have been damaged by them. Can't you perch somewhere else?"

"Ccccoooo, a perch is a perch," Big Ed replied. "Maybe *you* should stop building statues in *our* parks."

"Now, Ed, suppose we did that. We could take away the benches around the statues too. Then fewer people would come to the parks, and you know what that means — fewer handouts for you guys!"

Big Ed gave me a worried glance with his bright red eyes. Then he did a few flutters for me to remind me how pretty a pigeon can look in flight. When he came back, he cooed, "Gotta go now. I'd better mention this at an important meeting we're having — about a new statue being put up across town." As he flew away, he called back, "Thanks for the crackers!"

Suddenly a dog nearby began to bark. I woke up and thought about my dream. I smiled as I remembered Big Ed and his bluster.

Then I thought about all the thousands of dollars and hours people have spent trying to frighten pigeons away. Every big city has a pigeon problem, but nothing seems to get rid of them. *Maybe we should try to build pigeon-proof buildings where they can't roost,* I thought. But even if we did that, I knew there would still be plenty of pigeons around to watch. As Big Ed said, they sure do keep ahead of us.

Good stories do more than entertain. They teach, as well. From its first issue back in 1967, *Ranger Rick* magazine has distinguished itself by publishing hundreds of stories that capture children's imaginations—and teach them about wildlife, about ecology, about all of nature. We are pleased to reprint here some of the best of those stories about a rich variety of wild animals, from unfamiliar creatures in distant lands to familiar ones in our own back yards.

Library of Congress Cataloging in Publication Data

Main entry under title:

Ranger Rick's Storybook.

Summary: Twenty-seven stories, both fiction and non-fiction, about animals and nature.
1. Animals—Juvenile literature.
[1. Animals. 2. Animals—Fiction. 3. Nature —Fiction. 4. Short Stories] I. Ranger Rick's nature magazine. II. National Wildlife Federation.

QL49.R34 1983 813'.01'0836 83-8060
ISBN 0-912186-47-X

National Wildlife Federation

1412 16th Street, N.W.
Washington, D.C. 20036

Dr. Jay D. Hair
Executive Vice President

James D. Davis
*Senior Vice President,
Membership Development
and Publications*

Staff for this Book

Howard F. Robinson
Managing Editor

Victor H. Waldrop
Project Editor

Donna Miller
Design Director

Michael E. Loomis
Art Editor

Vi Kirksey
Editorial Assistant

Margaret E. Wolf
Permissions Editor

Priscilla Sharpless
Production Manager

Dolores Motichka
Pam McCoy
Production Artists